CU00657862

Best Wishes

Sandy

xxx

CAMPO

A guide to the Spanish countryside

Sandy Walker

SANTANA BOOKS

Copyright © 2005 Sandy Walker
The authors assert the moral right to be
identified as the authors of this work.

Designed by Chris Fajardo
Photography by J. D. Dallet

Campo - A guide to the Spanish countryside
is published by Ediciones Santana S.L.,
Apartado 422, 29640 Fuengirola (Málaga).
Phone 952 485 838. Fax 952 485 367.
Email: info@santanabooks.com
www.santanabooks.com

All rights reserved. No part of this book
may be reproduced or transmitted in any
form or by any means without the prior
written permission of the publisher.

Printed in Spain by Gráficas San Pancracio S.L.
Depósito Legal MA-904/2005
ISBN 84-89954-43-7

To Andy
who makes all things possible
~ and joyful

ACKNOWLEDGEMENTS

A million thanks to my daughter, Tam, for her continuing support — the endless hours over the years of information-gathering and nibbling away at the mountains of Spanish bureaucracy; and to Pete, Wednesday and Ella for their love, diversionary tactics in moments of stress and the joy that you all bring to my life.

Special thanks to:
Tai-chi-Pete for being one of the most interesting founts-of-all-knowledge.

The employees of the Ministerio de Medio Ambiente in Málaga and Madrid, some of whom were enormously knowledgeable and helpful and some of whom were obviously in training for promotion to the role of Events Manager, in particular, the paper-chasing and treasure-hunting events; I learned something from all of them.

The Ayuntamiento of Comares for advice and supplementary information.

Roberto for his advice and energetic support of the organic movement in Andalusia.

Cynthia for her support and professional input.

Norm for his wealth of agricultural knowledge.

Esta and Cheryl for help with the photographs.

Erica and Angus Watson of Magic of Andalusia who supported, encouraged and forged links to the outside world.

Not forgetting Peter Fitton. Many thanks for your feedback on the "pamphlet".

Y gracias a los buenos vecinos, José, Bernardo, Mari-Tere, Manuel y David, que nos han ayudado tanto durante nuestro tiempo aquí.

Muchas gracias por todo.

ABOUT THE AUTHOR

Following the hippy trail in the early 1970s, Sandy Walker lived in Crete and Italy before returning to England to bring up her daughter and run a business. After another period of travel she became a business adviser and qualified as a holistic aromatherapist. She moved to Spain in 1988 and bought a farm near Ríogordo amid the hills of Málaga province where, with husband Andy and daughter Tammy, she ran a holiday centre for yoga groups, bird watchers and art groups. Now living near the village of Comares, she is involved in building, yoga holidays, the land, her grandchildren — and writing.

Contents

INTRODUCTION

I lay in the dark listening to the first sounds of a new day penetrating the thick walls and heavy shutters. The wild north wind that had been blustering since the previous afternoon had moved on to disturb someone else's peace. When I first came to live in Spain, the force of the winter wind terrified me. There were nights when I slept on the floor in the kitchen at the front of the house rather than lie awake in the north-facing bedroom listening to the gales. Without any tall trees or buildings to resist their force, strong winds howled around the mountains in frightening gusts, bringing whispers of snow from the sierrras; winds of such strength that they were bound to ravage the landscape and reduce the flimsy cane roof of my *cortijo* (farmhouse) to a game of "pick up sticks". Yet, next day, I would wake to a still, quiet world, where trees and roofs remained stubbornly in place, as though a gentle summer breeze had kissed the landscape and the wind was merely the beating of a bird's wings.

I was unwilling to emerge from the warm bed into the unheated room. Three winters in Spain had taught me that the superb Andalusian climate did not extend to winter nights. Neither do traditional *cortijos* provide much protection, with their wonderful combination of cold, tiled floors, minimal heating and whistling draughts from wooden window frames and doors that grow and shrink faster than Alice in Wonderland. Apart from the day they are fitted, the windows and doors are always either too large or too small, wedged closed or allowing field-mice in to shelter in the kitchen or make their beds in the cosiness of coat pockets.

As the early-rising solo bird gathered a choir around it, I estimated that I had another 10 minutes before swapping the warm bed for the cold bedroom. The bedroom may not have been heated but at least it was dry and clean. A few winters living with old, leaking cane and mud roofs had soon cured my romantic notions of Spanish farmhouses. I chuckled when I thought of my mother's first visit to this house which I considered my own little piece of paradise. She was horrified at my rustic home, and particularly terrified of falling asleep on her back with her mouth open and accidentally swallowing one of the many bugs that dropped down from the old cane ceiling. Every night she attempted to sleep in a sitting position, propped up by countless pillows. Most of the ceilings were now replaced with new eucalyptus beams and good solid render between them. The joy of having a bedroom free from the continuous showering of wood-lice and dust was superb.

Breakfast over, I dropped my daughter at the school bus and, on an impulse, decided to take the dog for a walk. The arduous couple of years that we had spent rebuilding and extending the house meant that there had been little time for such pleasures and the dog had spent so much time running around the hillside with the goats that she was starting to believe she was a goat, too. Rebuilding the farmhouse had been a good learning curve, an experience I didn't particularly want to repeat, although at that stage I didn't know that I was to do it twice more (so far). Now the house was finished and beautiful, the piles of rubble pushed back and buried below patios and gardens. Gentle vines and passionately coloured bougainvillea were already scrambling over pergolas, spiky yuccas and palms exploded like fireworks around the periphery with jasmines and *dama de noche* patiently waiting to scent the warm summer nights. The closest I could get to paradise. The first yoga-holiday group was due to arrive in three days, followed by a couple of bird-watching groups and an art group. It was destined to be a busy spring.

Molly the dog and I walked down to the river and followed the mule track up the opposite hill. The sun was pushing warm rays through gaps where the ridges of the Sierra Tejeda were silhouetted against the pale-blue sky. I watched the light ripple across the neatly ploughed furrows which interspersed the rows of almond and olive trees. On it swept, down to the bridge and the stream, fringed with eucalyptus, and on further to illuminate rocky outcrops punctuated by caves surrounded by oaks. No matter how often I look at the Andalusian landscape, I never tire of its magnificence and, even after 16 years, it continues to inspire me. Years of living in Spain have not dampened my love for the country and the people. As the sun continued its ramble across the valley, I gazed across at my beloved home, expecting to see it nestling beautifully within its exotic greenery.

Great shock! The house was sparkling white, the immediate surroundings were green and lush, but everything else around it was a nightmare. Down the hillside shoulder-high weeds were competing with tree-suckers for space and light. Straggly, overgrown, mis-shapen olive trees looked extremely sorry for themselves and cried out for help. The first tiny almond blossoms were struggling to compete against last year's fruit, still on the tree and black with age. Between the trees, prickly pears marching with astonishing speed seemed to fill every available space. Alongside my neighbours' neat, well-tended groves this was a travesty. With shock and horror I realised this neglected, unloved piece of Andalusian paradise was mine. This was the patch of God's own earth that I was responsible for and I had failed to tend it and love it.

For three years I had been so busy with the house and its immediate environment that I had planted a garden and savoured the exquisite views with pleasure, but the surrounding land and indigenous trees were undemanding and had been left to their own devices. Three years of neglect had wreaked havoc, and I felt ashamed.

When I first arrived in Spain, my generous neighbours had offered help and advice. In true *campo* tradition they believed the land came first. You put all your energy into the trees, fields and animals and then, if there was any time left, you might consider painting a wall — or installing running water. Their approach was totally logical because their food and income came from these sources. However, unlike them, my income was not from the land but from rural tourism and my priorities were very different. I had been so occupied learning about cement, plumbing and electricity that it left no time to consider olives and almonds.

I was confident that I could retrieve the situation, but hadn't a clue how to go about it. I knew my neighbours would be only too willing to help, but I was ashamed and embarrassed at the extent of my neglect and ignorance. I trawled through my memory and reviewed exactly what I knew about farming in Spain — it took all of two minutes. I rushed indoors and dug out the one and only book on gardening in Spain that existed in English at that time, Marcelle Pitt's *Gardening in Spain*. When living in England I had never quite joined the gardening fraternity; growing nasturtiums in nasty weather or roses in the rain had never appealed. But in Spain I found the exotic plants with their fast rate of growth and vibrant colours completely fascinating. Gardening in Spain had become my gardening bible, even though it contained some quirky advice. For example, for the absentee gardener she suggests: "Best bet may be to get a gardener or maid to water your garden or planters once a week with a hose-pipe." Sadly, my maid happened to be on permanent leave. I looked up "Olive". Fewer than six lines offered some fairly basic information, i.e. olive trees don't need much water and are pruned in autumn. The section on almonds was slightly more comprehensive, particularly regarding the useful decorative effects of almond blossom within the home. I was getting the feeling that this might not be the practical reference source I required. What I needed was a solid body of information: what to chop off; when to chop it; what to do with it once I chopped it; did I need to fertilise it, if so when and what with…

I had no option but to approach my kind, bemused neighbours and admit ignorance. In the intervening 13 years I have learned a lot by trial, error and good advice. We moved house, acquired an old olive mill, more land and two beautiful granddaughters, and are still involved in rural tourism. Some years, due to pressure of work, the trees make their own sweet way without too much attention from Andy or myself, although we do try to consider their needs. More recently our quiet rural area has been "discovered" by several agents who have brought more *extranjeros* to the area and I often hear our Spanish neighbours lamenting the fact that foreign land-owners leave the land to revert to wilderness, that the plants are meaningless to them and it is a sad state of affairs.

Having been what I jokingly referred to as a "virgin olive-oil producer", I know how the incomers feel. I talk to many people who want to do something with their land but haven't a clue how to go about it. They don't know, and can't be expected to know, the way of the land or the laws of the countryside. Do hunters really have the right to hunt on your land? Is it true that people are allowed to help themselves to your wild asparagus (and what does wild asparagus look like anyway?). It's easy enough to harvest crops, but what on earth do you do with three tons of olives, a ton of carobs and several sacks of almonds?

I've waited 13 years for someone to write this book and now I'm fed up waiting. So here it is. I sincerely hope that it will prove interesting as well as useful.

CHAPTER 1

ALMONDS

Almond tree: *almendro*
Almond nut: *almendra*

Although some of the trees we encounter when we arrive in Spain may only be known to us by name, the almond, or *almendro*, being a relative of the cherry tree, is probably easier to recognise than most. Its stunning blossom, reminiscent of Chinese and Japanese paintings, is a familiar sight. The almond tree originated in the Middle East and Western Asia and experts believe that a semi-wild variety has been growing since pre-historic times.

The Hebrew name for almond is *shaked*, which translates as "early rising", and this embodies the nature of the almond tree, one of the earliest to blossom. In Spain, December heralds the first signs of new growth on the trees when the first flower buds emerge from the bare branches before the leaves. Across the mountains of Andalusia the numerous groves of almonds reach the peak of their beauty in January and, by the end the month, the countryside is awash with drifts of pink and white blossom. A blast of strong wintry wind blows petals like snowflakes around the hills.

Almonds are from the extensive *Prunus* family which includes cherries and plums as well as the shrubby sloe or blackthorn. They grow well in chalky, arid soil and, apart from many large-scale producers, most properties have a few almond trees scattered around the land. It can be very satisfying to harvest and dry your own almonds because they can be used in a wide range of recipes: roasted as a garnish, employed as flavouring in traditional dishes such as *pollo andaluz* (Andalusian chicken), or ground up to make a thickening agent for sauces and soups, for example the cold soup *ajo blanco*. As well as being delicious when fresh, almonds have the great advantage that, stored correctly, they keep well for a couple of years.

Almonds are harvested in summer, usually in August. They are ready for picking when the velvety outer husk starts to separate from the shell. The Spanish word for husk is *cáscara* but, locally almond husks are referred to as *capotes* or cloaks, easy to see why when you look at the split husk covering the inner shell. Almonds can be picked individually from the tree but, if you aim to harvest a whole tree or several trees, it is easier and quicker to collect them in the same way as olives, i.e. spread a large net or sheet under the tree and bang the branches, or the nuts, with a long stick. Almonds are heavier and harder than olives so it's not much fun if you are under the tree with the stick and nuts rain down on you. Wear a hat — it helps.

It is easy to remove the husk of a ripe almond. It should peel away without any problems, leaving a hard outer shell containing the nut, or *almendr*a (refer to the section on Harvesting). The nut itself has a thin, dark brown skin which can be slightly bitter. The easiest way to remove it is to blanch the almond in hot water for a few seconds, after which the skin should peel away without any problems.

Almonds may be quicker to harvest than olives but removing the nut from the shell can be a fiddly, time-consuming process. If you have a lot of trees with a high yield, you can purchase a machine to do this for you. However, if you have only a couple of trees, you probably will do it yourself. The traditional method is to hold the nut in one hand on a wall or flat rock and bang it hard with a stone. This isn't as easy as it sounds and you may suffer a few bruised fingers before you get the knack. The real skill lies in hitting the almond hard enough to split the shell but leave the nut intact. It can be a little disheartening sitting with a group of local women who are methodically working their way through a sack of almonds, neat piles of nuts and shells beside them, while you are chasing after nuts that shoot across the countryside every time you hit them. After 15 minutes of this entertainment you accumulate a small pile of almond crumbs and sore fingers and are tempted to go indoors and find the nut crackers. However, you soon get the knack and merrily bash away with the best of them, confident that you have accomplished a new skill — until next time you try when you find you have forgotten everything you learned and are back chasing around the fields after flying nuts. Maybe it's best to secretly use the nutcrackers in the privacy of your own kitchen.

Once you have a large pile of almonds, shells and husks, what can you do with them? All parts of the almond are useful. The outer husks are fed to goats and mules. Broken shells are burned in open fires, wood-burning stoves or *braseros* (those metal dishes containing glowing coals placed under Spanish tables). They also make good mulch for the garden. The nuts can be eaten raw and, if you have only sampled those bought in packets from supermarkets, you will find the soft, buttery texture and taste of fresh almonds are incredibly different. In fact, the fresh nuts are so soft in texture that they make "butter", a good, home-made alternative to real butter.

Your harvest may yield several kilos of almonds, but be careful not to over-indulge. When we were first almond-bashing with our neighbours, they were very keen to impress upon us that eating too many at one sitting was bad for the digestion and would result in stomach ache. Thinking that this was in keeping with the general belief that over-indulgence in anything is not a good thing, I was surprised to discover that the warning went deeper and that almonds can be extremely toxic. Some almonds, along with the kernels of many other fruits, such as apricots and plums, contain amygdalin which breaks down into cyanide. Suddenly the tales of Hercules Poirot and Sherlock Holmes, where the smell of almonds leads them to conclude that the victim has been poisoned with cyanide, start to make sense. However, do not panic. Some sweet almonds do not contain any amygdalin and others contain only trace elements of the chemical and are harmless. Bitter almonds have much higher amounts, hence

the very bitter taste (nature's built-in warning), which makes it extremely unlikely that anyone would want to eat more than one or two. The obvious question is: how do you recognise bitter almonds? The answer: by appearance alone, with difficulty. The nuts look very similar, although bitter almonds tend to be slightly flatter than the sweet variety. The best solution is to taste them. A nibble on a bitter almond will be

enough to put you off eating any more. Because of their toxicity, it is recommended that young children should NEVER eat bitter almonds.

On the plus side, research is producing some excellent results in favour of almonds. Amygdalin, commonly called laetrile (or vitamin B17), was first isolated in 1830 in Russia, where it has since been used to treat cancer. As cyanide is believed to be an active cancer-attacking element of lactrile, dispute about its use continues. However, in the field of nutrition almonds receive a very favourable press. Dieticians have long been concerned about nuts in our diet because of their high oil content, but there is growing support for almonds because almond oil is low in saturated fats and contains many nutrients, such as calcium and magnesium, which aid the growth of strong bones and the prevention of osteoporosis. Compounds in almonds are claimed to protect us against heart disease and cancer. Not only are the nuts cholesterol-free but most fats in almonds are mono-unsaturated, which are believed to help reduce cholesterol levels. They are one of the best sources of vitamin E: a mere three ounces of almonds will provide 105 per cent of the recommended daily allowance. Vitamin E is a powerful antioxidant and some studies have shown that antioxidants may help to fight cancer. Almonds also contain folic acid, recommended for those contemplating pregnancy. In fact, it can be said that almonds are one of the most beneficial and nutritious nuts available.

The good news is that almonds store well so once you have harvested them you will have a supply to keep you going throughout the winter. They are best stored in their shells until required and will keep for a couple of years but remember you will have a crop next year… and the year after. If you want to sell them, the easiest way is to contact your local co-operative to see if you are registered or your nearest commercial producer. Most factories will accept small amounts (one or two sacks) for processing, but the price per kilo is currently quite low and, unless you have large quantities, it probably isn't worth the time and expense driving to the factory. The highest prices are commanded by marconi almonds which are round, very hard and larger than the average almond.

Almonds are sold on to the food and pharmaceutical industry. They are used to make marzipan or sugared almonds and the oil is employed extensively in the beauty industry, as well as being the predominant oil used in massage and aromatherapy. The light oil is less viscous than most and easily absorbed into the skin, so it is frequently used as a carrier or base oil for massage, to which essential oils are added. In Spain you will rarely see almond oil on supermarket shelves, either in the culinary or beauty section. The place to buy it is at the chemist's. *Aceite de almendras* is usually stocked in large quantities and can be bought by the litre, or the pharmacist may fill a smaller bottle for you.

If you have a lot of almond trees, more nuts than you can handle and do not want the bother of selling the produce, consider having some of the trees grafted with other fruits to give you a variety. We have very successfully grafted plums on to some of our almond trees. Grafting is quite a skill. If you are knowledgeable about plants, you can attempt it yourself, but there will usually be a local expert to perform the task for you.

In late summer, once the tree has produced its fruit, it loses its leaves but many of the nuts will remain firmly attached to the tree unless harvested. During autumn the husk will turn black and look fairly unsightly, moreover the presence of the nut will inhibit flowering in the spring. Even if you do not want the crop of almonds, it is advisable to knock the nuts from the tree. Failure to do so over a period of years will result in the slow decline and eventual death of the tree.

In Spain at Christmas you cannot avoid noticing the massive displays of *turrón* that invade supermarkets and local shops alike. As mince pies are to the UK, *turrón* is to Spanish people. Originally made from almonds and honey, *turrón* is apparently of Jewish-Arabic origin and there are references to it in literature of the 14th century. Rivalry still exists between Catalonia and Alicante as to where exactly it was first made. Today a vast selection of *turrones* mixed with an assortment of chocolates, nuts and liqueurs is available and various types come from almost every region. A basic recipe at the end of the chapter awaits you to add all your favourite ingredients and develop your own particular brand of *turrón*.

Cultivation

Botanical names: *Prunus amygdalus, Amygdalus communis,*
variety *dulcis* (sweet almond), variety *amara* (bitter almond)
Height: 8m (26ft). Spread 8m. Hardy down to -9C.

Likes well-drained soil and high summer temperatures. No
watering in summer once established. More drought-resistant
than most fruit trees. Flowers appear in December and January
before the leaves and the blossom is either white or pink.
Most are self-sterile so two different varieties must be planted
together for fertilisation to occur. The flowers give way to
velvety-covered green fruit which splits open when ripe to
reveal an edible nut. Almond trees normally have a short life
span (60-70 years).

Pruning

Almond trees need pruning to stimulate good crop production.
Prune after harvesting in late summer or early autumn. Remove
any dead wood or diseased branches and any branches that
cross or rub against other branches as these will wound the
tree. The wood is hard and sweet smelling, wonderful when
burned on an open fire.

Harvesting

Harvest in summer when the husk around the nut starts to
split open. Remove the outer husk, which should pull away
quite easily. Spread the almonds out in the sun for a couple
of days to dry out. To test for readiness, shake the almonds.
When you can hear the nuts rattling inside the shells, they
are ready for eating or storing. Once dry, the almonds can be
stored in a cool dry place for a couple of years without
deteriorating. They are best stored within their shells.
Failing to remove the fruit from the tree for several years will
result in the decline of the tree.

Pests And Diseases

All the *Prunus* family are susceptible to a fungus called peach leaf curl, identified by the leaves turning a lovely shade of red which, on closer inspection, prove to be small red blisters. For further information on this, plus gummosis and bacterial canker, refer to Chapter 18 - Pests and diseases.

RECIPES

Turrón de guirlache

>500g (1.1lb) sugar
>a few drops of lemon juice
>500g (1.1 lb) raw almonds peeled.
>2 tablespoons sweet almond oil

Heat the sugar in a heavy bottomed pan with a few drops of lemon juice. Stir gently with a wooden spoon to prevent sticking. When the sugar has melted, add the almonds and stir until golden. Pour the almond oil on to some grease-proof paper to prevent sticking and then pour on the contents of the pan. Grease a rolling pin with almond oil and roll out the *turrón* until it is 1.5cm (3/5in) thick. Before it has completely cooled, cut it into strips.

Ajo blanco

A cold almond and garlic soup, deliciously refreshing on a hot summer's day.

>250g (8oz) almonds
>155g (5oz) white bread with crusts removed
>2 cloves garlic, peeled
>salt
>155 ml (5fl oz) olive oil
>1 tablespoon sherry vinegar
>1 litre very cold water

Blanch the almonds for two minutes in boiling water, drain and rub the skins off. Soak the bread in a small amount of water. Crush the almonds, bread, garlic and salt in a mortar and pestle or food processor. Drizzle in the olive oil. Add the sherry vinegar, then the cold water. Refrigerate. Check for seasoning and serve well chilled. The soup can be garnished with white grapes if so desired.

CHAPTER 2
CANE

Cane: *caña común*

Cane *(caña)* is a fundamental part of life in the Spanish countryside. Farmers have traditionally used it as a handy building material, fast-growing and light to transport. Cane looks very like bamboo. Tall and graceful, with lush green foliage and brush-like flowers, it sways elegantly along the edges of fields and rivers, its drying leaves rustling in the breeze. Like bamboo, it is a grass but, whereas bamboo is a tree grass, *caña* is actually a giant reed called *Arundo donax*. The main differences between bamboo and cane lie in the internal structure of the culms, or stems, but externally you will be able to differentiate the two by their leaves. Cane leaves, like those of sugar-cane, sprout straight from the central stem. They alternate their way up the cane in the young plant, only in later years putting out branches, whereas bamboo has a complex branching system.

Extremely fast-growing, in the right conditions cane may rise to more than two metres in height during the first year. The canes are unusually flexible, and tend to curve when they grow very tall. *Caña* grows in clumps or rhizomes which look rather like large pieces of ginger as they spread outwards. A delightful clump grows around a ford in our local river, which acts as a natural car wash when we drive through it.

This ancient reed is native to the Mediterranean area. Some of the numerous references to reeds in classical literature and the Bible are believed to refer to *Arundo donax*. Although mainly used to create musical pipes, in many countries this reed has been most useful for building. Modern methods and materials have replaced many old building techniques but traditional building materials remain readily available and are usually cheap or free. In Andalusia the traditional way to roof a house is to tie canes together and lay them across wooden beams which are covered with a layer of mud. On top of this go roof tiles. However, this method can be time-consuming and, as we're usually short of time and better off than in the past, it's easier to phone for a delivery of concrete roof beams.

Many years ago my husband, Andy, and I bought a 300-year-old olive mill. The fact that it had no windows, few doors, very little roof and — in some places — even less wall did not deter us. Although I could say that we were young with romantic visions, in fact we were probably old enough to know better but we still had romantic visions. The land stretched down to the river-bed and contained two natural springs, one surrounded by ferns and looking so grotto-like that Bernadette of Lourdes would have felt at home there. The mill, which retained all the old pressing and milling equipment, nestled within a thicket of bright red geraniums as high as the roof, and slumbered quietly in the afternoon sun. It was Sleeping Beauty waiting to be awakened and restored to life and we knew we wanted to do the kissing. The whole project was not helped by the fact that the mill did not have any road access but there was a mule track through a neighbour's olive grove. We intended to restore the building using traditional building methods and, as there were thousands of rocks scattered around for walls and our land along the river contained eucalyptus and cane, what more could we want?

We intended to do most of the work ourselves and restoring this little corner of Andalusian history would be a labour of love. We made a couple of rooms habitable and moved in. One of the first jobs we undertook was to build a roof over what is now our sitting-room. We cut the eucalyptus and cane and left them to dry. We gazed lovingly, like proud parents, on our little wigwams of drying cane and waited patiently to get on with the job. It so happened that Andy had to visit England just when the beams were in place and the cane was ready. He was only going on a short trip so I planned to strip the cane of its sheathes, leaves and branches and cut it to the correct length so that we would be ready to proceed when he returned. Andy rootled around among the tool store and came up with a few potential cane-stripping instruments that he considered I might be safe with.

Although I am generally extremely competent, when I have accidents I have them in a big way. Only a couple of years earlier I had dropped an ash tray on my foot, severing an artery, which led to blood poisoning, gangrene, six months in a wheel chair and the risk that I would spend the rest of my life hopping about. Knowing the havoc I could wreak with a mere ash tray, Andy did not intend to leave me alone with a sharp instrument. In fact, he seemed less than happy to leave me with anything sharper than the plastic surgeon's knife in our grand-daughter's doctor's kit. However, after a few cane-stripping moves, I realised that the job could be done easily only with a sharp tool. If it was a little blunt, it would lodge itself firmly in the base of the branches and removing it could be dangerous.

Our neighbour José wandered along to see how we were getting on and ambled off, returning 10 minutes later with a small, razor-sharp machete. Andy paled visibly, but I was thrilled because the whole process was much smoother and easier with this exquisite tool. Before heading for the airport, he organised a rota of people to visit every few hours during his absence to make sure I hadn't done the unthinkable. I grabbed the machete and surveyed my wigwams. The whole job should take one-and-a-half days, I judged — a ludicrous assessment considering I had never stripped any quantity of cane in my life. I grabbed the first piece of cane and started swishing with the machete. It was so satisfying peeling away the crisp brown sheath and dead branches to reveal the golden cane underneath — at least it was for the first two hours. At the end of the first day I was mind-numbingly bored. What's more, I had a huge pile of dead leaves and branches, very few golden staffs and it seemed as much cane waiting to be stripped as I had at the beginning of the day. Day two showed some progress, days three, four and five passed in a blur. But at long last the job was done and the canes were cut to length awaiting Andy's return. It took us a further three days to put them securely in place across the roof beams, at the end of which we surveyed the ceilings waiting to be restored, picked up the phone and ordered a delivery of concrete beams. To this day the sitting-room remains the only room in our mill with a traditional cane ceiling.

Short pieces of cane are also used under roof tiles to give them extra support and when strung together to make "rafts" they can be employed in a variety of structures. In many countries these rafts form internal walls, a much quicker and easier construction method than building with stone. Once the cane walls are in place, they are plastered.

Apart from cane's usefulness in the countryside, it has been used across the world in aesthetic ways, particularly in the field of music with a history stretching back more than 5,000 years. Very early references abound to *Arundo donax* being used to make musical pipes and reeds and today it remains the main source of reed for woodwind instruments, such as clarinets, oboes, saxophones and bagpipes. Cane's suitability for musical reeds lies in the combination of flexibility and resilience within the culm. Many experiments have been made to produce musical reeds from alternative materials, particularly during the two world wars when large quantities were cut and woven into screens to camouflage troops from the enemy, leading to a scarcity of reeds. But, so far, no other material has achieved its quality.

France is the main producer of musical reeds, particularly the area around Fréjus. Perfectionists theorise endlessly about the factors affecting the quality of the reed: the type of soil it grows in, the ambient climate etc, and insist that reeds from other countries are inferior to those from France. However, experiments have demonstrated that this may all be in the mind. In tests, most musicians considered reeds they believed to be French were of superior quality to others; in fact, they were using reeds from cane grown in other countries, including Spain.

Making musical reeds seems to be a long-winded process

(excuse the pun). Selected canes are cut when they are two to three years old and left to dry. The time allowed for drying varies greatly between plantations and is often determined by the reed manufacturer that the harvest is destined for. The reeds are tied into bundles and stacked in wigwam structures. Over a period of two to four months the moisture from inside the cane disappears, then the outer sheath and leaves are removed. The leaves are frequently sold on as animal bedding. The canes are cut into lengths, slightly longer than a metre, and then left in the sun to cure. They are turned regularly so that they dry evenly, becoming a uniform shade of gold. Makers' recommended drying times for reeds vary tremendously. Some advocate six months to a year, others insist that a longer drying period is essential. Production techniques vary, but opinion seems unanimous regarding the diameter of the bamboo and its suitability for reeds of different instruments. For example, a reed for a clarinet is produced from canes with a diameter of 2.5 cms (6ins.) while that of an alto-saxophone is from a 2.85cm (7in.) cane.

Cane is also utilised in the production of paper, materials and medicines. *Arundo donax* has a very high cellulose content, which makes it particularly important in fabric production. Cellulose extracted from the cane is treated with sodium hydroxide and carbon disulphide to produce a viscous, orange-brown solution, subsequently regenerated into rayon fabric. An ambitous project in Italy, before the Second World War, had mixed results. Mussolini, attempting to make Italy self-sufficient, encouraged a large textile corporation to plant acres of cane in the province of Venice with a factory to produce cellulose pulp for fabric. The original farm was established on marshy wasteland and the 6,000-acre site was projected to expand to 15,000 acres by 1943. The factory aimed to produce 40 per cent of Italy's requirements. One useful by-product of the production process arose from the high natural sugar content in the cane which converted into alcohol. Each ton of pulp produced 54 gallons of 95 per cent ethyl alcohol, important in the field of medicine. The eventual success of the project is open to interpretation. Some sources say that the quality of the cellulose produced was not of high enough standard and therefore spurned by rayon manufacturers. Although the factory achieved some success, reports attribute this to the use of cheap timber imported from Yugoslavia. Using cane in paper-making has had mixed results. Large-scale projects in Argentina and France fell by the wayside when other raw materials became easily available.

Cane is very versatile and is traditionally used in a wide variety of everyday objects such as walking sticks, fishing rods, baskets, plant supports and chair seats. Split-cane can be woven into rolls and used for screening, fencing or shade. Despite the decline in its use for building, great swathes still grow around the countryside. One of its prime functions is the prevention of land erosion. Cane is as effective in retaining the banks of swollen rivers during periods of torrential rain as it is in holding back large areas of drifting sand and has been used throughout the world to prevent erosion.

Cane also has its applications in local folk medicine. Mainly the roots are used. An infusion is recommended for dropsy, for regulating both high and low blood pressure and for reducing fever. Boiling the roots in wine and adding honey to the liquid is suggested in the treatment of various cancers.

Besides being useful, cane is also pretty. Both the leaves and the flowers are decorative, and not just out in the fields. The tall, white, fluffy flowers have long been popular and particularly in the 1970s they were often dyed and used for interior decoration. If you don't have any other use for your cane, I can thoroughly recommend a tall culm as the ideal instrument for removing cobwebs from high ceilings and inaccessible places. Just remember to cut it when the flower-head is young and strong and thus unlikely to scatter seeds everywhere.

Cultivation

Botanical name: *Arundo donax*
Height: 2-5metres (6-16 ft). Tolerant down to –7 degrees C.

A genus of six species native to the Mediterranean. A giant

reed which spreads rapidly in wet places. A perennial with a rhizome root system which produces woody stems resembling bamboo. Canes have an outer leafy sheath, green when young turning brown. The canes are green when young and turn gold as they mature. Flat, green, elongated leaves grow alternately along the stem on young canes and direct from slender branches on older canes. Grows best in full sun and tolerant of most soil types, even sand.

Flowers

Tall, slender, fluffy flowers appear in late summer which are usually white but shade through to green.

Irrigation

Cane grows best in moist conditions but will survive short periods of drought. It can easily be established in moist soil but will become established in other places with watering.

Propagation

Difficult to propagate from seed. Propagate in autumn or spring by dividing the rhizome (root).

Harvesting

Theoretically the canes can be harvested at any time of year without damaging the rhizome, but the best time to cut it is autumn through to spring. It should be cut when the moon is waning. Local people say that cutting cane when the moon is waxing and the sap is rising causes men' testicles to swell up, but I haven't found anyone willing to test this theory. If you have to cut cane in summer, be careful: it contains high levels of silica which can spark and create a fire hazard. If you are growing cane as a windbreak or to create privacy, it is best to cut the whole clump back to the ground at the end of each year because the new growth has the densest, greenest leaves. If growing it for decorative flowers or to use the canes, leave for a second year.

Uses of cane

Screening or shade: For screening or shade, whole stems of cane look better and last longer than the split screens sold by garden centres and agricultural suppliers. Cut the cane in spring and stand it to dry for a week or more. Then strip off the sheath, leaves and any branches. Use sturdy gloves for this as cane splinters are extremely painful. Cut the canes to the required length and weave them into rafts with wire.

Plant Supports: Cane can be used for supporting plants but bamboo is sturdier. Cut the canes and leave them to dry. Strip away the outer sheath and leaves and cut to length. Once cut, the cane can be stored for a long time. It will not be damaged by rain. If you store it without removing the sheaths, they will dry and become mottled causing discolouration in the cane. If you have cut your cane to stimulate new growth and have no other use for the pieces, break them into small lengths. They make excellent kindling.

CHAPTER 3
CAROB

Carob tree: *algarrobo*
Carob pod or bean: *algarroba*

Arriving in Spain for the first time, many of us vaguely
recognise an olive or an almond tree but have only the
tiniest notion of what a carob is or what the tree may look like.
Yet this is a fascinating tree with a rich history. It has been
cultivated throughout the Mediterranean for more than 4,000
years. Large and shady, with dense dark-green foliage and
long, dry-looking brown pods, the carob prompts more
inquiries from our visitors than any other tree in the valley.
They generally know little about carobs and their usefulness
and are surprised to discover that the pods, and the beans in
them, are used in a variety of well-known products, such as
tinned pet food. I was amazed when my father recognised
carobs and remembered eating them as a child in the 1920s
in Scotland, where the pods were sold alongside liquorice roots
in the local shop.

You won't see many groves of carobs but their dark shapes
dotted here and there around the landscape are easily
recognisable. Most *fincas* have a few scattered among the
olive groves and usually one growing quite close to the
house. Those dark, inedible-looking pods are a rich source of
nutrition and traditionally grown in Spain as animal fodder
although they became a dietary staple for humans during
periods of famine. Carob trees seem to be few and far between,
so it is surprising to discover that Spain, with 4 per cent of total
production, is the world's largest producer of carob beans.

The tree is evergreen with a twisting trunk which is often
hollow and filled with a dark brown powder, the residue of

leaves and pods. This powder is such a good source of nutrients for the soil, for fertilising and mulching, that it seems endowed with magical properties. Unusually, carob pods are attached to the branches of the tree rather than on lateral stems. The pods begin their life green and look similar to runner beans, not surprising when you realise that the carob tree is a member of the legume family which includes peas and beans. Throughout the summer, the pods lengthen, harden and turn chocolate brown as they ripen. The description "chocolate brown" is very apt as carob is one of the main chocolate substitutes used in the health food industry and can be found in health food shops as a powder for cooking or in a variety of "chocolate" bars and drinks. Carob is a rich source of sucrose, protein, minerals and iron and has the advantage of being virtually fat-free, with only 44 per cent of the calories of chocolate. It is also non-allergenic and doesn't contain any caffeine, which makes it a good chocolate substitute for migraine sufferers. If you fancy a quick snack while wandering around the *campo*, the ripe pods are edible straight from the tree. However, they are extremely chewy, very sweet and seem to last forever in your mouth.

Fully-grown carob seeds, inside the pod, are all reputed to be of similar weight and were once the standard measuring device used by goldsmiths. A piece of gold was weighed against a set number of carob beans and, through centuries of general usage, the word "carob" evolved into "carat" as in nine, 18 or 24-carat gold.

In some countries carob trees are also called locust trees, the beans being "locust beans" or "St John's bread". There are several references in the Bible to locusts and I remember, as a young child, being particularly disgusted by the story of John the Baptist eating locusts and honey in the desert. It was a relief to discover that the locusts referred to were not insects but locust beans (hence St John's bread).

As well as producing food from the pod, carob is in great demand for its seeds, from which is extracted the natural food additive locust bean gum, or LBG, a glutinous substance used extensively in tinned pet food. Spain is one of the largest producers of LBG with more than half the world's processing factories sited here.

Most of us are not aiming at large-scale carob production but have a few trees and hate to see the produce go to waste. So what can we do with them? The pods are extremely messy lying all over the land or patio and need to be collected anyway, so why not knock them off the tree and gather them into sacks? If you have animals (although I'm not sure your cat or dog would relish them) or a neighbour with animals, you don't have a problem. Country folk value carobs as nutritious food for their goats and mules. You may have a neighbour willing to harvest the beans and prune the tree in return for the produce, but this is becoming less likely as families shrink in numbers and often have enough on their hands with their own harvest. We have a dozen carob trees which we harvest and distribute among friends and neighbours with livestock. Throughout the year our Spanish friends are extremely generous with their time and the produce from their land. As they are almost self-sufficient, it is difficult to give them anything meaningful in return, but free animal fodder always seems to be appreciated.

If you are keen to produce your own healthy alternative to chocolate, try the recipes at the end of the chapter. Whether or not you are motivated to collect the pods, it is easy to enjoy a carob tree. On a hot summer afternoon it is a treat to rest in the tree's wonderful cool shade and indulge in the romantic notion of generations of local *campesinos* enjoying a *siesta* in just such a place, surrounded by goats and a mule feasting on the wholesome convenience food.

Cultivation

Botanical name: *Ceratonia siliqua.*
Height: 8m (26ft). Spread: 10 m (33ft). A genus of only one species. A relatively fast-growing tree that can reach 6m in 10 years. It likes full sun, although in warm areas it will grow well in shady conditions. Requires well-drained soil. Resistant to frost down to –5C, but this is one of the few trees that suffers in

the wind. The stems are very brittle and break easily in strong winds.

Flowers

Trees are either male, female or hermaphrodite, and it is impossible to tell which until the flowers appear. Female trees have the highest yield of fruit. The most common practice for establishing carob orchards is to graft selected fruit on to seedling rootstock, but if you are only buying one or two carobs for your land the supplier should be able to tell you what type of tree you have. The trees start bearing fruit when they are 6-8 years old. In winter and early spring 15-cm (6in) racemes of small flowers appear directly on the old wood. The flowers are both wind and insect-pollinated and have a pollination period of several months.

Harvesting

The seed pods reach 20-30 cm (8-12 in) long and are ready for harvesting in late summer. Although large-scale carob growers are experimenting with mechanical harvesters, most *campesinos* with only a few trees harvest them by hand using the same method used for olives and almonds, i.e. spread a net under the tree and bang the tree with a long pole. Speaking from experience, I find carobs considerably easier to harvest than olives. Being large and dry makes them easy to gather; the sacks fill up satisfyingly quickly and are much lighter to carry when full — all great bonuses as far as I'm concerned.

Once harvested, the carobs should be stored in hessian sacks, not plastic as this makes the pods sweat and rot. The carob crop can vary tremendously. One year you will get a fantastic crop and hardly anything the next. This highly variable flower and fruit production within orchards and between years creates particular difficulties for farmers and industrialists producing crops on a large scale. Research suggests that the presence of pods on the tree inhibits flower production and therefore the following year's crop, so to produce the maximum crop it is important to remove all the pods. Other factors can affect crop production, but research has so far failed to provide the answers.

Watering

The carob has a very deep root system. This makes it extremely resistant to drought so that, although 50cm (20in) of rain annually is ideal, a tree will still produce a crop with less than 25cm (10in). Demand for carob beans coupled with its ability to resist drought mean that countries with arid zones, like Australia, are considering large-scale plantations and carobs are planted prolifically in reforestation programmes throughout Spain.

Pruning

Prune the tree in autumn after the crop has been harvested and before the flower racemes appear. Carob branches tend to be quite brittle and break easily. Remove any spindly branches and dead wood. Knock off any pods still clinging to the branches in order to encourage next year's crop. The wood from carob trees is extremely hard and a beautiful red colour. It looks too beautiful to burn on the fire but produces a lot of heat.

RECIPES

Carob Flour

Wash pods and remove seeds. Place the pods in a pressure cooker for about 20 mins at 15lbs of pressure. Allow to cool. Process in a blender until you produce a powder. This can be substituted for chocolate in any recipe.

Carob Cake

1/2 cup butter
1/2 cup honey
1/2 cup dark molasses
1 egg

1/2 teaspoon cinnamon
1 teaspoon baking powder
1/3 cup carob powder (see above)
2 cups whole wheat flour
3/4 cup hot water
1 cup chopped walnuts

Heat oven to 250C. Beat butter, honey and molasses together, add the egg and beat again. Sift dry ingredients into the bowl, alternating with hot water to loosen the mixture. Stir in the walnuts. Pour into a lightly greased cake tin and bake for about one hour. When cool it can be topped with carob frosting or, if that sounds too healthy, use real chocolate topping.

Carob Frosting

2 tbsp butter
2/3 cup powdered milk
1/3 cup carob powder
1/4 cup honey
4 tbsp cream
1 tsp vanilla

Cream butter, powdered milk and powdered carob together to make a thick paste. Add honey and cream. Mix. Add vanilla and whip until smooth.

CHAPTER 4

CITRUS FRUIT: ORANGES

The range of citrus fruits and the vast number of different fruits within each category merit a book on its own so I have restricted myself in this chapter and the next to two main types — oranges and lemons.

Months at sea on long sea voyages to distant continents subjected sailors to a scourge known as scurvy and massive numbers of men died from the dreadful disease. But ultimately the problem was identified as a vitamin deficiency which could be alleviated by eating citrus fruit. British sailors consumed vast quantities of lime juice to stave off scurvy, earning them the nickname "limeys". How many of us growing up during the 20th century received dire warnings over our breakfast orange juice and marmalade that if we didn't consume it all we would get scurvy? It was enough to put you off your breakfast.

Citrus fruit has played a large part in the economy of Spain since the first commercial plantings near Valencia in the 18th century and now citrus groves cover vast tracts of land in Valencia and Alicante and on through southern Spain. In fact, more than 272,000 hectares of the country's land are dedicated to citrus farming and Spain is the world's fourth largest producer with more than five million tons per year, 60 per cent of which is exported, mainly to the rest of Europe.

Following two centuries of rapid commercial development, the 20th century witnessed some of the greatest changes in citrus production and, as is often the case, the biggest change was stimulated by disaster. Just as wine production was thrown into crisis during the late 19th century by the *phylloxera bug*, citrus groves fell victim in 1956 to an outbreak of *tristeza*, a viral disease which almost put an end to citrus production in

Spain. *Tristeza* translates as "sadness", but the disease could more aptly be named "tragedy". It causes yellowing of the leaves and stunts the growth of trees, eventually leading to their death. As with vines affected by the *phylloxera*, citrus groves were saved by the identification of a rootstock resistant to infection and a huge campaign was undertaken to graft varieties of citrus on to these rootstocks. Following the disaster, the government established various bodies to research and improve citrus production. In 1975 the Citrus Variety Improvement Programme of Spain was established. One of its objectives was to develop virus-free plants and supply them to commercial nurseries. The first of these plants were offered to commercial orchards in 1981 and the programme proved successful.

An interesting aspect of Spain's commercial citrus production is that 80 per cent is bought "from the tree". Adverts that portray an inspector from a well-known orange juice producer examining the fruit and saying "Yes" are not so far from reality. Growers and buyers have a direct relationship, with visits from the buyer commencing when the tree is in flower. The crop is assessed at this stage, the harvest is forecast and arrangements made for each subsequent stage of the process. The person responsible for monitoring the crop assesses the tree at various intervals and counts the fruit-lets, not an easy task. At specific points in its growing cycle the fruit is measured and the tree is checked for pests and diseases. Citrus growers are particularly aware that the crop must be well manipulated to ensure the highest level of production and, with this in mind, a regular programme of pruning and thinning of blossom and fruit-lets is undertaken. Compared with many trees, citrus do not have a long life and, when grown on a commercial scale, they are usually dug up after 20 to 25 years and replaced. Luckily citrus wood makes excellent firewood.

Spain has more than 500 packer-exporters and the industry is a major source of employment. Think of the vast number of products from citrus fruits, not just fruit and juice, and you begin to comprehend the importance of the industry. Marmalade, liqueurs, essential oils, ascorbic acid, the list goes on… thank God for resistant root stock!

ORANGES

Fruit: *naranja*
Tree: *naranjo*
Orange grove: *naranjal*

The perfume pervading the air from a grove of orange trees in blossom has to be one of the most heavenly natural fragrances available to us mere mortals. Pure and unadulterated, the scent lingers on the evening air and clings to clothes — orange trees offer a perfume that stimulates a maximum "feel good" factor. We all know the sheer pleasure of juicy ripe oranges, freshly squeezed orange juice, delicious tangy marmalades and rich soothing orange liqueurs. Something about the scent, taste and colour of an orange makes one feel better about life, particularly on a cold, wet, grey day in England. It's a sort of sunshine take-away. It is unsurprising, therefore, to discover that the essential oils contained in the tree's fruit, leaves, blossom and roots all contain wonderful healing properties. Whereas many trees and shrubs, such as eucalyptus or rosemary, contain oils that heal the body and the mind, essential oils from orange trees also heal the spirit.

Oranges are full of vitamin C and an excellent source of fibre but, in addition, the essential oils — contained in the peel, the blossom and the tree — are some of the most potent available in aromatherapy. Oils from the peel of the fruit, easily seen by the naked eye, can be released by simply squeezing some peel between the fingers. This oil is produced commercially by large-scale pressing of the peel. In fact, the peel is so rich in volatile oils that many *campesinos* dry it for use as a natural fire-lighter.

The leaves and twigs of some varieties of orange (most notably the bitter orange, *Citrus bigaradia*) are also full of essential oils and the oil distilled from these is called "petitgrain". *Petitgrain* oil was originally produced from very small unripe oranges, no larger than cherries, hence the name "small grains". However, this proved commercially unviable because it considerably reduced the potential crop of mature oranges and nowadays production is mostly restricted to distillation of leaves and young twigs.

Essential oil produced from the distillation of orange blossom is called Neroli and is considered to be the queen of essential oils. Surprisingly, this wonderfully fragrant oil is not distilled from the blossom of sweet oranges but from those of bitter Seville oranges. Neroli was named in the 16th century after Anna Maria de Tremoille, a princess of Neroli in Italy who used the oil extensively to scent her clothes and bath water. Today it is one of the most expensive essential oils available. However, it is extremely potent and usually only requires one or two drops to be effective. Neroli oil has powerful antidepressant and relaxing qualities and is used in the treatment of stress, nervous conditions, bereavement, or any type of emotional trauma. A by-product obtained in its distillation is orange-flower water. This became extremely popular during the 17th and 18th centuries because it is much cheaper but with similar properties to Neroli, though less potent. The Spanish word for orange blossom is *azahar* and the products are similarly named e.g. *agua de azahar* (orange-flower water) and *aceite de azahar* (orange-flower oil). Orange-flower water was once used throughout Europe as a body rub, or infused into water and drunk to cleanse the blood and overcome nervous afflictions.

Commercial planting of oranges in Spain began in earnest in the 18th century, making orange-flower water cheap and readily available for the home market. The demand was considerable, particularly from Madrid prostitutes who used it liberally. But in northern Europe oranges remained rare and expensive in the 18th and 19th centuries and were considered a luxury. The landed gentry built "orangeries" adjoining their stately homes to provide a supply of the luxury fruit, although many orange trees were grown simply for ornamental purposes. Some orangeries are still in evidence today, frequently converted to cafeterias in houses open to the public. Because of the high price and scarcity of oranges they were not widely used in the medical field, although an infusion was sometimes recommended to Victorian women who suffered from "the vapours" to assist relaxation and help steady their nerves.

Despite the prolific use of the flower water by Madrid prostitutes (or maybe because of it — who knows what Victorian gentlemen got up to on their Grand Tours and the ideas they returned home with?), orange blossom evolved into a symbol of purity and is traditionally used at weddings to adorn brides. The weaving of orange blossom into bridal bouquets and head-dresses is not simply decorative. Not only does the scent of orange blossom have a relaxing effect, it is an aphrodisiac — both properties which may have assisted nervous virgin brides, or even those Madrid ladies and their clients.

Spain's first commercial orange plantations were in the provinces of Castellón and Valencia. Now the east coast and Andalusia are the largest producers, differing varieties being produced depending on the various micro-climates. Bitter oranges from Seville are too sour to be eaten raw and are grown commercially for marmalade or orange liqueurs, but the cooler climate in Valencia is perfect for sweet, juicy oranges and clementines. This may seem surprising because many people associate oranges with hot climates, but while they need sunshine to stimulate strong growth they require cool weather to ripen. Think about your orange tree and you will realise that the fruit starts to ripen in autumn when the weather is getting cooler. The peel of the fruit contains an orange pigment which is released by cool weather. Mature oranges fail to turn orange in very hot countries and, even when ripe, they will remain green. Even more surprising is the fact that, in countries where heat and cold fluctuate rapidly, ripe fruit which has already turned orange will revert to green. To overcome this problem, commercially grown oranges are sometimes treated with ethylene to ensure uniformity of colour.

If you live in the Spanish countryside, it may seem rather pointless to grow oranges because once they are in season your neighbours will probably give you vast quantities. But there is something so magical about the sight of an orange tree and the scent of its blossom that it is well worth growing at least one tree simply for the perfume and the visual feast of those sunny globes nestling amongst the dark glossy foliage.

For details about cultivation, see next chapter.

Oranges and aromatherapy

Orange oil: Oil is expressed from the skin of both sweet and bitter oranges. Caution: all citrus oils are photo-toxic and should not be used on the skin immediately before going into direct sunlight or any UV light.

Neroli: The oil distilled from the blossom of the bitter orange tree. Anti-depressant, aphrodisiac, hypnotic, sedative and soothing, uplifting. An effective balancing oil for skin, assisting both oily skin and dry mature skin.

Bathing: four to eight drops in bath water late at night will aid sleep by eliminating tension and restlessness. For shock or grief, add three drops of oil to almond oil and massage into the back and chest in a clockwise direction. Neroli is such a gentle oil that it can be used safely on children and pregnant women.

CHAPTER 5

CITRUS FRUIT: LEMONS

Fruit: *limón*
Lemon tree: *limonero*
Lemon grove: *limonar*

Lemon trees are believed to have originated in India and to have reached Europe in the second century via Greece, where lemon was used mostly as an insect repellent and perfume for clothes. Virgil refers to the lemon as the "Median apple" because it came from Media, an ancient kingdom corresponding to modern Azerbaijan and Kurdistan. From Greece, lemon trees spread through Italy and reached the Iberian peninsula around the fifth century AD.

Of the thousands of plants and vegetables used in pharmaceutical products, lemons are one of the most effective for healing and purifying. Although we think of lemon juice as very acidic, it becomes alkaline within the body and produces potassium carbonate, an effective antacid to treat indigestion. The scent of lemon has long-held associations with cleanliness, that lovely sharp citrus smell so frequently synthesised in cleaning agents. Therefore it comes as no surprise to discover that lemon is an effective antiseptic and bactericide which also whitens and bleaches. The tradition of squeezing lemon juice over fish is not simply about flavour: experiments have shown that a few drops of lemon juice can kill 92 per cent of the bacteria in oysters in just 15 minutes, so you could be doing yourself a favour by squeezing lemon on your food. In places where the cleanliness of the water may be suspect, adding lemon to the water, in the ratio of the juice of one lemon to one litre of water, will help to purify it. A simple way to extract the maximum amount of juice from a lemon and make it easier to squeeze is to soak it in water for 10 minutes before you use it.

The purifying properties of lemons are well known by country-dwellers, who use them not only for food or drink but to cleanse, whiten and soften. Lemons are excellent for whitening and softening skin, particularly good for cleansing the hands after a rough day working on the land. Lemon juice is also used to bleach cloth and is an effective natural cleaner for bathrooms and kitchens. Every cook knows that squeezing lemon over cut fruit and vegetables, such as apples, avocados and bananas, helps to slow the browning process and retains the natural colour of the fruit.

Perhaps lemon juice's most amazing quality is its ability to cleanse and regulate blood. It reduces blood's viscosity and stimulates the circulation. Lemon is so powerful that it makes *tuberculosis bacilli* inactive and stimulates white corpuscles in our blood (those are the goodies that help us to fight infection). Essential oil of lemon neutralises *staphylococci* bacteria in approximately two hours, so the treatment of sore throats and colds with lemon and honey is not only homeopathic and traditional but extremely effective. Lemon juice is a good tonic for gums and, because it stops bleeding, it is an effective mouthwash after the trauma of a tooth extraction. So far I have failed to discover an ailment, in either humans or animals, that the local people don't treat with lemon juice, olive oil, honey, or a mix of all three.

This amazing little fruit is not only a stimulant for the body. Increasingly, research is demonstrating lemon is an effective mental stimulant that improves intellectual performance. Lemon oil stimulates the hippocampus area of the brain and increases our ability to memorise facts. Japanese researchers burned lemon oil in offices and recorded a substantial 54 per cent reduction in typing errors. So burning lemon oil in an incense burner will not only purify the air that you are breathing but may improve your mental agility.

As with most citrus oils, essential oil of lemon is produced from the skin of the fruit and no fewer than 3,000 lemons are required to produce one kilo of essential oil. Surprisingly, the unripe fruit produces more oil than the ripe yellow lemons. Once the peel is removed, the pulp of the fruit is used to produce citric acid and the peel is also used in the food industry, for example, boiled with sugar to produce candied peel.

Although they grow fairly prolifically here in Spain, lemon trees are not as hardy as oranges. They are more tolerant of wind but very susceptible to frost damage. It is worth finding a sheltered place in the garden to grow a lemon tree and, if you can find a good position, sheltered from the wind, the tree will reward you with a copious amount of fruit. Some varieties of lemon (such as *Luna*) produce fruit and flowers all year and it is estimated that one lemon tree can produce 3,000 lemons in one year. The problem of what to do with all this wonderful fruit will not be helped by your neighbour kindly dropping in every other day with another bag of their surplus crop for you. I do not think that there is any soft drink on the market that can match the taste of homemade lemonade, but there are only so many gallons you and your family can consume. You may even suffer a significant drop in the number of visitors popping in when the large, bottomless jug keeps appearing from the fridge.

Then you could have a brainwave: lemon curd. You dig out the old family recipe and are shocked to discover that a single lemon makes several jars of the stuff and what's more you also remember that you never liked it anyway. A couple of good-sized lemons do seem to go on and on. In Morroco they deal with the problem by preserving them. Preserved lemons have a very subtle, delicate flavour which adds a distinctive note to Morocco & Morrocan cooking. The peel as well as the flesh is edible and full of flavour.

Over the years, as you become used to the plentiful fruit your well-tended trees produce, you may feel less guilty about leaving lemons rotting on the ground. It has been sad to witness the decline in lemon groves during the last few years in Andalusia. Many farmers are replacing them with more lucrative crops such as avocados and mangos. Subsidies to farmers are such that many harvest their crop of lemons but consider it a waste of time to sell them so that it is not uncommon to see lorry-loads of lemons dumped in river beds. Despite the glut, it is well worth growing at least one lemon tree for the sheer pleasure of walking outside and picking a lemon direct from the tree whenever you need one. The fresh flavour in your gin and tonic or lemon tea is unbeatable, but there are also the delights of lemon sorbet, lemon cake, lemon meringue, lemon and gin sauce... the list seems endless.

Cultivation – oranges and lemons

Botanical names: lemon - Citrus *limonum (rutacae)*; Seville orange - Citrus *aurantium;* sweet orange - *Citrus sinensis*

Propagation

Citrus trees are fairly easy to propagate and this can be done from either seeds or cuttings.

Cuttings

Take 10cm (4ins) cuttings from an established healthy plant and place them in sandy soil. Water regularly until the roots become established and you can see new growth before transplanting into the ground.

Growing from pips

Select very fresh pips and do not allow them to dry out. Wash them thoroughly to remove any pulp which may adhere to the pips causing them to become mouldy. Use a soil-based compost and push the seeds down so that they are just below the surface but completely covered in earth. Water thoroughly and keep in a warm place. Seedlings should appear within three weeks and will be ready for potting-on when they reach 15-18 cm (6-7in) high.

Transplanting

Although citrus trees can be successfully grown in pots, they will provide a better supply of fruit if planted in the ground. If you do wish to grow them in pots, use unglazed clay pots in preference to plastic ones because this allows more air through to the roots.

When transplanting trees, take great care with the roots. Lemon trees in particular have very sensitive and brittle roots which break easily, so be careful not to damage them. Lemons are not as hardy as oranges and do not like frost. In cooler areas the tree may become dormant so plant your lemon tree in a warm sunny spot. A bout of frost will cause the tree to lose its leaves, although many trees will survive the occasional blast of cold. Citrus trees can be planted at any time of year but are likely to respond best if you plant them in spring once all danger of frost has passed. Dig a hole as deep as the root ball and twice as wide. Citrus trees hate being water-logged so make sure that the soil drains well. When you fill the planting hole, make sure that the soil level does not come any higher than the level of soil that was in the original pot. Covering any more of the stem will make the tree more susceptible to disease. Water regularly until the trees are established.

Watering

Citrus trees like lots of water but do not like to be water-logged. Once established, they prefer a cycle of flooding and drought, rather than drip irrigation, although I have read that many commercial growers successfully use drip irrigation. Dig a hollow around the base of the tree extending as wide as the branches and flood this with water and then do not water again until the soil has dried out. As a rough guide, give each mature tree 10 litres of water every 10 days.

Pruning

Citrus trees do not require much pruning, but it will help to strengthen the tree if you thin some of the branches out, particularly any that may be crossing or rubbing against others and causing damage. It is easier to access the fruit if you keep the tree fairly low-growing, particularly some varieties of lemons have very sharp thorns. Healthy trees will produce more fruit than you can possibly manage to juice, squeeze or add to a gin and tonic, so you can afford to remove some of the tiny emerging fruit to stimulate the production of larger healthier fruit. The best time to prune the tree is in early spring when all fear of frost has passed.

Pest and diseases

Of all the trees growing on my land, I have found citrus trees the most susceptible to pests and diseases. There was a time when I found it a constant battle; either something was eating the leaves, they were yellowing, becoming sticky, or curling, or the stems were infested with little white woolly creatures. I was at the end of my tether, but the trees continued to survive and produce good crops of fruit. Experience has taught me that, more than anything, citrus trees need vigilance. If you only have a few trees, it is easy to check them every week and aim to deal with any disease or pest as soon as it strikes. Apart from the usual collection of aphids and ants, some of the main pests that attack citrus trees are the citrus leaf miner, spined citrus bug and, if you see lots of small white balls like cotton-wool clinging to the leaves or branches, these are most likely to be mealybugs. These pests will sometimes bring infestations such as sooty mould. Further information on pests and diseases, and how to deal with them, in Chapter 19.

RECIPES

Preserved Lemons

> *1kilo (2.2lb) small lemons, preferably thin-skinned*
> *salt*
> *12 fl oz lemon juice*
> *1-2 tbsp olive oil*

Cut from the pointed end of the lemon down towards the stalk, but do not cut through the stalk. Do this so that the lemon is in quarters but still joined at the stalk end. Gently open each lemon and pack it with salt. Place the lemons in a preserving jar and put a weight on top of the fruit. Leave in a warm place for a few days, by which time some juice should have accumulated in the bottom of the jar. Top this up with lemon juice until the lemons are completely covered. Pour olive oil on top to seal it and prevent mould from forming. Put the lid on the jar. The liquid will start to clear and the lemons will be ready for use in about one month. If they have been correctly prepared and completely covered, preserved lemons will have a shelf life of two years.

Lemon and gin sauce

This traditional recipe was first published in 1877, the peak of the gin-drinking era in the western world. It is so easy to make and delicious poured over steamed puddings. Use the peel and juice of as many lemons as you like. For the peel of each lemon add 3 tablespoons of sugar and a cupful of water. Simmer gently for about 20 minutes. Remove the peel and add the juice of the lemons to the pan. Add a measure of gin to suit your taste and gently reheat the sauce, without boiling it, when you are ready to use it.

CHAPTER 6

EUCALYPTUS

Eucalyptus: *eucalipto*

As you look over the Andalusian landscape with its neat almond and olive groves, eucalyptus trees are immediately identifiable by their completely different shape and character. Tall, lush and elegant, they sway like willows along folds in the landscape and fringe the banks of dry river-beds. Groves of eucalyptus offer shade from the searing summer heat and their pungent aromatic scent pervades the evening air, heady and evocative. Walking through the leaves and shredded bark that carpet a eucalyptus grove is a walk through incense.

Eucalyptus, or gum trees, are usually associated with their native Australia and koala bears, but in the past 200 years they have become true giants among the trees of the world. They were first brought to the attention of the western world in 1770 by Joseph Banks, the British botanist who accompanied Captain Cook on his travels to the Pacific, but it was a further 19 years before the genus was described and named. The French naturalist Labillardiere brought the trees to Europe in 1793, but it was not until 1846 that the first eucalyptus arrived in Spain, in Galicia. It spread from Spain to its South American colonies. Although originally considered an ornamental tree, its usefulness and desirability lay in its extremely fast rate of growth and tolerance of a wide variety of climatic conditions. Its ability to thrive at high altitudes meant that the eucalyptus proved invaluable in countries such as Ecuador, Bolivia and Peru. It provided wood for building and furniture-making in conditions where it was considered impossible for any tree to survive.

The range of properties and the uses of eucalyptus seem

endless. These adaptable trees appear worldwide in every-thing from reforestation programmes to paper and clothing production, from highly effective medicines to the roofs of Spanish farmhouses. They are one of the world's most important (if not the most important) hardwood timber resources. However, ecologists in Europe have recently voiced considerable opposition to eucalyptus plantations on the grounds that the trees completely suppress plant growth around them and support very little in the way of insect life, although this may seem difficult to believe on a hot summer afternoon when your eucalyptus tree is humming loudly and irritatingly with thousands of insects and bees.

There are more than 500 different species of eucalyptus, some being small garden specimens and some growing into the tallest trees imaginable. So large is the range of flower colours and tree sizes, plus the variety of leaf shapes, that a species can be found for practically every situation. Around the Mediterranean the commonest species is *Eucalyptus globulus*, known as the Tasmanian blue gum, which is planted throughout the Spanish countryside for its timber. Look at the ceiling in your farmhouse or that of your neighbour and you will usually see a variety of timbers, but the chances are that most of the beams will be locally-grown eucalyptus planted by a previous generation. When you wander around the hillsides of Andalusia and see a grove of eucalyptus alongside a grove of cane, you know that a roof has been planted for the next building project. As a roof beam, *Eucalyptus globulus* has the distinct advantage of being extremely fast growing, reaching a height of up to two metres in its first year. It is also ideal because the wood is durable and resistant to damp. The beams will be easily recognisable as eucalyptus because they have a tendency to split lengthways, but this does not seem to affect the strength of the beam. Once eucalyptus wood has been seasoned it is extremely hard, as anyone trying to hammer nails into it will discover.

The foliage of about 20 species, including *Eucalyptus globulus*, produces essential oils, now extracted on a commercial scale for the pharmaceutical and perfume industry. Oils are extracted from leaves, both young and old, by a process of steam distillation. Eucalyptus citriodora has a lemon-scented leaf utilised by the perfume industry, the broad-leafed peppermint eucalyptus *(Eucalyptus dives)* is in demand by the food industry and the Tasmanian blue gum is grown commercially for the pharmaceutical industry being used in a range of products including soap, toiletries, medication and insect repellents. To many of us, the scent of eucalyptus evokes memories of childhood illnesses: blocked noses and wheezy chests treated with oils and vapour rubs. Many of these remedies are still used today. Along with China, the Iberian peninsula is one of the world's largest producers of eucalyptus oil.

The use of eucalyptus as an antiseptic and healing oil is well known in its native Australia where a eucalyptus grove provides a walk-in pharmacy for Aborigines. Eucalyptus leaves burned in sick-rooms release essential oils which fumigate the room. Scientific testing has established that a spray containing as little as two per cent essence of eucalyptus can kill 70 per cent of ambient *staphylococci*. Without the benefit of scientific evidence, the Aborigines know that those with respiratory illnesses benefited from sitting close to burning eucalyptus leaves and inhaling the healing smoke. Those suffering from asthma or bronchitis roll dried eucalyptus leaves into cigarettes and smoke them, the original menthol cigarette. The leaves have been used to treat internal ailments but also to treat external problems such as wounds, inflammation and burns. Leaves exude oil with antiseptic qualities and, when wrapped around affected areas, stimulate healing and the renewal of skin tissue. As well as medicines, eucalyptus roots provide a lifeline to Aborigines during periods of famine and drought. When all other sources of water dry up, long lengths of eucalyptus root are dug up and vigorously blown into, producing a liquid at the end of the root which is collected and drunk, the roots then being dried and eaten.

Eucalyptus truly complements the whole spectrum of life. As well as being fundamental to building, medicine and furniture-making, the tree adds to the arts. This is the tree from which didgeridoos are formed. The instrument is created by termites when they eat their way through a limb of a tree, producing a hollow pipe. During the 19th century eucalyptus became known as the "fever tree" because it was believed to ward off malaria and other fevers. This was not just superstition. Eucalyptus have very thirsty roots and are now deliberately planted in boggy, swampy areas to dry them out. As well as reducing swamps of stagnant water and depriving the dreaded mosquitoes of their breeding ground, eucalyptus trees exude a scent which deters mosquitoes from breeding around the tree. Every home should have one.

Cultivation

Botanical name: *Eucalyptus globulus*
Height: 40-60m (132-198ft) with a spread of 10-25m (33-82ft). Two distinct leaf forms: young trees have broad silvery leaves while older trees develop long, thin needle-shaped leaves (it is easy to mistake young and old trees for different species). A messy tree with heavy leaf fall and bark that strips away from the tree, leaving a silvery blue-grey trunk. Can reach two metres in its first year and continues to grow quickly, often reaching heights of 60 metres (198ft) in temperate and semi-tropical environments.

Planting

Eucalyptus globulus can be grown easily from seed and indeed one of its invasive properties is that it sets seed easily wherever it grows, forming groves of eucalyptus in a very short time. Although the seeds of *Eucalyptus globulus* take two years to mature, the trees are best grown from seed because established plants do not transplant well. If you are tempted to steal a march on time and purchase a tree from your local plant nursery, be aware that the older the tree the greater the difficulty it will experience in transplanting. In particular, do not buy any tree that is root-bound in its pot because it will experience problems when transplanted in forming a root system sufficiently strong to provide the anchorage and support required by a fast-growing tree.

Sow mature seed in early spring with the seedlings as far apart as possible. Bear in mind the trees' ability to grow and spread quickly. If you are transplanting a young tree, the top of the root ball should be 3-4 cm (1-1.5in) below ground level in a shallow depression. As well as providing a dip to hold water for the sapling, this protects the swollen base that develops on eucalyptus. This base (the lignotuber) is capable of producing new shoots from dormant buds if the main stem is damaged and will assist a transplanted tree to start again. In autumn fill the depression with soil. *Eucalyptus globulus* is tolerant of most soil types and prefers a very sunny position. As with most young trees, staking is important in the early stages, particularly if you are growing eucalyptus in a windy area. Preventing wind-rock while the roots are establishing themselves is crucial.

Once established, the trees need very little summer watering although the tree has a reputation for being very thirsty. Its invasive roots absorb any available water and hold on to it, leaving no water for any other vegetation to grow around it. Its wide-ranging roots can damage foundations and it is generally recommended that the tree should be planted a minimum of 6m (20ft) from a wall.

Flowers are produced in spring and early summer, either singly or in clusters of two or three and reach a width of 4cm (1.5in). These are followed by blue-grey seed capsules.

Problems

Although eucalyptus is fairly resistant to pests and diseases the tree has a tendency to suffer from chlorosis. If the leaves start turning yellow, treat with an iron supplement.

Pruning/pollarding

The pruning method depends on whether it is to be grown as a tree, a bush, coppiced for screening, or pollarded for beams. Eucalyptus generally produce new shoots from both the base and the stem and therefore a variety of pruning techniques is suitable, depending on your requirements. Coppicing annually is a simple and effective method of growing eucalyptus in small gardens. This contains the tree at a height and shape suitable for a smaller environment. However, in the countryside pollarding is the more usual system of pruning. This method encourages the tree to push out new shoots or "legs" which should result in several shoots around a central trunk growing to the desired length. This is ideal for providing wood for building because it encourages many fast-growing shoots rather than one very thick trunk.

To pollard the tree, encourage a main stem (or leg) to a required height and then cut all growth back to this level. Select the strongest shoots, evenly spaced around the trunk, to grow and cut away all others in March or early April. Continue pruning back any weak shoots. When the selected shoots have reached the height you require, cut them off at the point they emerge from the main trunk. The tree will quickly produce new shoots and repeat the cycle.

To coppice the tree, when the tree is in its second year of growth, cut back the tips of side shoots to prevent them becoming dominant. In third and subsequent years, cut back the stems close to ground level. Feed with 1oz per square metre of sulphate of ammonia and mulch with well-rotted compost or manure.

PRODUCTS

Timber

In Andalusia eucalyptus wood destined for beams is traditionally cut in January or February, but only when the moon is waning. Once cut, the beams need to be left to dry before being used. *Campesinos* often leave beams lying on the ground where they fall until needed. If you see lots of large beams lying around looking abandoned, rest assured that they are simply waiting to be moved to their final resting place. The beams will take at least two or three months to dry depending on the weather and are often left for up to a year.

Eucalyptus makes good firewood but again leave the beams to dry before using on the fire. The high oil and resin

content in eucalyptus means that the logs burn well, but the oils exuded can be a problem in wood-burning stoves, the cooling effect of the chimney producing a rich unguent which may ooze through joints in the chimney pipe. This looks disgusting and can be difficult to remove.

MEDICATION

Leaves

Most of us are probably unlikely to offer our children or grandchildren a home-rolled eucalyptus-leaf cigarette for their asthma and would choose to buy their medication from a pharmacy or homeopath, but if you are keen to tap into the natural eucalyptus remedies you could try distilling oil from the leaves. This method of extracting essential oil is the same for most cultivated or wild plants that can be found growing in the countryside, including lavender and rosemary. Information on using eucalyptus oil is available at the end of this chapter and further information on aromatherapy and essential oils is contained in Appendix 1.

Infusions

The stimulating properties of eucalyptus help to combat nervous exhaustion and tiredness. To make a stimulating drink, add two or three leaves, or one tablespoon of chopped leaves, to boiling water. Boil for one minute and leave standing to infuse for 10 minutes. Strain off the liquid and add sugar or lemon if desired. Caution: Do not use pure essential oil of eucalyptus in drinks. It is too strong to be taken internally and can prove toxic to the system.

Eucalyptus and aromatherapy

Eucalyptus oil is widely used in aromatherapy and homeopathy and the essential oil can be bought from many outlets. The following information is a guideline for using the oil and the conditions for which it may be appropriate. Eucalyptus oil is an extremely strong oil and should NEVER be used on babies or very young children.

Uses

Eucalyptus oil
- has pain-relieving properties and is antiseptic
- is particularly useful in respiratory problems and urinary tract infections
- heals wounds
- reduces fever
- combats infections
- has a revitalising, stimulating effect on the body and nervous system
- when massaged into the skin, will help to alleviate pain associated with rheumatism, muscular aches and fibrositis
- along with geranium and juniper, has an ability to lower blood sugar levels and is useful in the treatment of diabetes

Applications

Steam inhalation: for flu, bronchitis and respiratory disorders, blend four parts eucalyptus oil (10-15 drops) mixed with two parts thyme, two parts pine oil, one part lavender. Place the oils in a bowl of hot water, make a tent over your head and the bowl with a towel and inhale the vapour.

Massage: for massaging the skin, eucalyptus oil must be added to a carrier oil of your choice. Those most commonly used in aromatherapy are almond, sunflower, olive, avocado and coconut. These oils can be blended to suit your skin, or use an alternative oil of your choice. If you find the scent of eucalyptus too overpowering but desire its healing properties, you can successfully blend it with the following essential oils: lemon, lemon-grass, lavender or pine. The blend of oils can be inhaled, massaged or added to bath water to ease aches and pains associated with fever.

It is important to note that essential oils are strong substances and undiluted oils should NEVER be applied directly to the skin. This is particularly important in the case of children where undiluted oils could cause severe skin irritation. Essential oils must always be mixed in a carrier oil at a ratio of sex drops per 5ml for adults and two drops per 10ml for children. Certain strong oils, such as eucalyptus, should never be used on babies or young children.

CHAPTER 7

FIGS

Fig tree: *higuera*
Early fig: *breva*
Ripe fruit: *higo*

Fig trees are one of the most wonderful trees growing semi-wild. The fruit can be picked and eaten straight from the tree without all the husking-drying-marinading involved in preparing olives or almonds. Not content with producing beautiful fruit, the trees are real *prima donnas* and naturally spread into weird and wonderful shapes with twisted, curved branches reaching and curving as gracefully as the arms of ballet dancers.

Fig leaves are traditionally associated with modesty, a connection weaving back to Adam and Eve. The leaves have been utilised in numerous works of art to save many a coy maiden's blushes, but in reality fig trees have preserved modesty and provided clothing in the South Sea islands for centuries — and not just the leaves. In the Philippines, Indonesia, Papua-New Guinea and Malaysia, cloth is produced from the bark of various trees, including fig and mulberry. This bark cloth is called *tapa* or *kapa*. To make it, the bark is harvested when the trees are small, only 5-8cm (2-3in) in diameter, and placed in running water for several days, after which the outer layers are scraped away, leaving a fine inner fibre which is beaten to the required texture and thickness. Not only is the resulting cloth described as being incredibly soft, it is considered cooler than any cloth produced in the western world.

The process of beating *kapa* was observed by Captain Cook and the naturalist Joseph Banks on their first voyage to Tahiti in 1768. They brought samples of the cloth home with them and described it as being equivalent to the finest muslin available. Once the cloth was made, it was dyed and again the fig was utilised in the process. A shade of red, which Banks described as "more delicate" than any colour encountered in Europe, was produced by mixing the sap from the fruit stems with the leaves of various other plants such as convolvulus or solanum to produce a gentle scarlet colour. Bark clothing has the great advantage of being recyclable. When it wears out, it is simply combined with another batch of bark and pulped into a new garment.

The fruiting fig found growing around the Mediterranean is the common fig, *Ficus carica*. Figs are a member of the mulberry family, *Moraceae*, and the genus *Ficus* contains 750 different species. However, considering the extent of the genus, there are very few species that provide fruit. Most are utilised as ornamental trees and for shade. The well-known rubber tree, *Ficus elástica*, is one that is in common cultivation as both house plant and garden tree. Vélez-Málaga in the Axarquía district of Málaga province, has what is believed to be Europe's oldest grove of rubber trees, providing an avenue of shade from the fountain at Calle Blas Infante through the Parque de Andalucía. This grove is an impressive sight, not just because of the height and spread of the trees but also because each aerial root has grown to the size of a small tree trunk and the grove resembles elephants "walking" along the avenue. However, Vélez-Málaga's rubber trees are totally upstaged by one of their relatives in India. Near the city of Poona, a *Ficus benghalensis* (otherwise known as a banyan tree) is reputed to have a spread measuring 606 metres (2,000ft) and it can shelter an estimated 20,000 people at one time.

The mention of fig leaves in the Book of Genesis is not the only religious relationship with the Ficus family. A species called *Ficus religiosa* is venerated by both Hindus and Buddhists. The Hindu deity Vishnu is believed to have been born under *Ficus religiosa*, commonly known as the "bo" or "peepul" tree, and Gautama Buddha spent six years meditating beneath the cool shade of the bo tree on his path to enlightenment.

Although most trees in the family do not produce anything edible, many members of the species provide useful products other than clothing and paper. In fact, the Ficus could be considered a type of general purpose tree. *Ficus elástica* is well known for producing latex and was the original source of India rubber produced extensively in Assam in the 19th century. Carpenters in Africa use the leaves of two native species, *Ficus exasperata* and *Ficus asperifolia*, as sandpaper because they contain a large amount of abrasive silica. Similarly, in the Philippines the leaves of *Ficus odorata* are used for scouring. A long way from its religious associations, the banyan tree produces a resin which was widely used in the manufacture of hair sprays and is still employed by some companies today. In general, wood from Ficus trees is unsuitable for building. Although occasionally utilised for posts and fencing, the wood is brittle, not very durable under moist conditions and has no commercial use.

Many figs start their lives as guests on other trees (epiphytes). Seeds dropped by birds or fruit bats fall to rest in the crevices of bark. Although they lodge in trees, figs are not parasites and do not feed off the host tree, a type of bed but not breakfast. Initially, they live on whatever nutrients the rain provides or any organic matter their roots may find. As they grow, they produce strong roots that grow towards the ground, each one reaching the size of a trunk. Frequently, the fig ends up completely strangling the host tree.

Although they have remarkably different growth habits, all figs are amazingly similar in their floral structures. In the past it was impossible for fig trees to produce fruit without the assistance of fig wasps which live and breed in the flowers and transfer pollen from male to female flowers. This was a problem because fig trees are capable of growing in climates that the wasp cannot tolerate, but it was solved when a hybrid fig was developed which set fruit without the need for pollination. Figs have very thin skins which creates difficulties in transporting the fruit, particularly when they are ripe. Nature compensates for the fact that figs do not travel well with the bonus that they dry very well and, like many other fruits, the dried fruit is more nutritious than the fresh fruit. Of all the fruits for sale in our local market, I always think figs look particularly wonderful, each fruit carefully wrapped in its own protective leaf.

Cultivation

Botanical name: *Ficus carica*
Height 7m (23ft), width 9m (30ft). Ficus are generally evergreen trees, but the edible variety of fig is one of the few deciduous members of the family. Leaves are 10-20cm (4-8in) long with 3-5 lobes. Fruit appears in early summer, 5cm (2in) long, pear-shaped, green when young, ripening to yellow-green or purple depending on the variety. It is a hardy tree requiring very little attention. Fig trees are virtually indestructible (while writing this I was disturbed by an escaped donkey and discovered he had eaten every single fruit from one of our fig trees but without doing any damage to the tree). They will survive well with little attention and very light pruning but attention will be needed to achieve a good crop of fruit.

Planting

The phrase "between a rock and a hard place" comes to mind when planting figs. They grow and fruit better in shallow soil and when their roots are confined. Finding a good site for a fig tree is not a problem in eastern or Mediterranean countries where pockets of arid, stony soil are numerous. In the UK figs were traditionally planted in brick pits one metre square to contain the roots. If planting the fig in a pot, restrict the pot's diameter and put a layer of stone and rubble at the bottom of it. Although the tree will survive at temperatures as low as eight degrees below freezing, anything below –4C will stunt the tree, killing the branches, and the tree will remain a small shrub that will not produce fruit. Plant the tree in a position where it will receive full sun. Figs like warmth, as much light as possible and soil with a high lime content. They can be difficult to grow in a mixed border because they do not like as much water as many other plants, neither do they like fertilisers rich in nitrogen.

Watering

To produce the best crop, figs like well-drained soil and will survive without any summer watering. Do not water when the leaves have dropped and the plant is dormant. Over-watering when the fruit is forming may cause the fruit to drop prematurely. Similarly, too much water when the fruit is ripening will result in fruit that is soft and tasteless.

Fruiting

In some countries figs will produce three crops a year. In Spain there are frequently two crops but sometimes only one, depending on climate and growing conditions. If you have successfully grown figs in cooler climates, you will notice a difference in the flowering and fruiting habits between cultivated and wild figs. Wild fruit take almost a year to grow and ripen, their embryos appearing in late summer on the leaf axils of short shoots and ripening into mature figs during the following summer. A second crop of fruit may develop on new growth during the summer. If these have not grown and ripened by September, they must be removed to allow further embryos to develop.

Fertilising

Once established, fig trees require very little fertiliser. They do not like soil that is rich in nitrogen or nitrogen-rich fertilisers.

Pruning

Trees can be pruned after fruiting and it is generally easiest to do so after the leaves have fallen so that you can see the state of the branches and the shape of the tree. Little pruning is required. Pinch out the tips of young shoots to encourage stronger growth. Prune away any dead wood or broken branches, reduce any crowded areas of the tree to allow light and air to circulate. Cut away any branches that are crossing and generally shape the tree into an open bush.

Propagation

Many mature fig trees have branches that reach the ground and form their own root system where they touch the soil. It is easy to propagate figs from these branches and you can peg branches down to the ground to encourage them to develop new roots. Keeping the new roots moist is essential to keep them alive. When pruning the tree, rooted branches can be cut away from the parent plant, left to rest in their rooted position for a few weeks and then dug up and planted separately. Cut back any excess growth from the new shoot in order to retain a balanced shoot.

Drying figs

Dried figs store well and have a higher nutritional content than fresh figs. Figs dry easily in hot weather. Simply spread them out in the sun and turn them frequently so that they dry evenly. If you prefer to dry them indoors (fewer problems with wasps), you can leave them on a warm, sunny windowsill or string them together and leave them hanging in warm air.

RECIPES

Many of my neighbours make fig cake, pan de higos, a variety of which can be bought in supermarkets throughout Spain. It is simple to make, needs no cooking, tastes delicious and has the added advantages of using some of the never-ending almond crop — and keeping the children occupied for 20 minutes! There are various recipes, some of which include the addition of alcohol - usually anise. However, if you are planning to offer it to children, the following recipe is fairly popular.

Pan de higos

> 2 cups chopped dried figs
> 1/2 cup blanched almonds, crushed
> 1 tablespoon icing sugar, or crushed almonds, to coat.

Pound the figs and almonds to a rough paste and shape into whatever shape you desire. Locally it is formed into sausages shape, but commercially is often shaped into round cakes. Once rolled to shape, coat it in crushed almonds or icing sugar. Wrap it in foil and refrigerate until chilled. Keeps for ages, but is so tasty that it probably won't last for very long.

Fig chutney

> 500g (1 lb 2oz) light soft brown sugar
> 1.25 litres (2 pints) red wine vinegar
> 1 kg (2lb 3oz) firm, slightly under-ripe black figs, cut into 1cm (1/2in) thick slices
> 500g (1lb 2oz) onions
> 250g (8oz) stoned dates
> 150g (5oz) fresh ginger root finely shredded
> 2 tbsp sweet paprika
> 1 tbsp white mustard seeds
> 3 tbsp chopped fresh tarragon or 1 tbsp dried tarragon

Put vinegar, sugar and salt in a preserving pan. Stir until the sugar and salt have dissolved. Bring to the boil and simmer for about five minutes. Add figs, onions, dates and spices. Bring to the boil and simmer for one hour until the mixture has thickened. Remove from the heat, add tarragon and mix well. Ladle into hot sterilised jars and seal. It will be ready for eating in one month and has a shelf life of one year.

CHAPTER 8
OAKS

Cork oaks: *alcornoques*
Holm oaks: *encinas*

Mighty oaks have been revered for centuries and are a traditional symbol of strength. Their hard, durable wood has been invaluable for building houses, ships and railways, making furniture and barrels, but one particular species of oak has proved fundamental to the economy of the Iberian peninsula: *Quercus suber*, the cork oak. Cork oak forests cover large tracts of land in the west of Spain and throughout Portugal. These forests are an invaluable asset to both countries, not only for the cork they produce but for the wildlife they support, among which are Imperial eagles and the Iberian lynx. The area around the Spanish-Portuguese border provides ideal growing conditions for oak trees, which thrive in very wet weather and enjoy the plentiful rain that blows through this corridor from the Atlantic. Fortunately, oak trees also tolerate drought and the extreme heat that the area experiences.

Cork oak forests cover no fewer than 2.2 million hectares (5.4 million acres) around the Mediterranean, of which 30 per cent is in Portugal and 20 per cent in Spain. Portugal produces 50 per cent of the world's cork, a figure which underlines the importance of this industry to the Iberian peninsula. For centuries these forests have supported a large itinerant workforce, called *corcheros*, who live in the forest throughout the harvesting season, usually from May to the end of August. However, the 20th century witnessed a decline in demand for cork as plastic bottle-stoppers increasingly replaced cork. Many ecological groups worked hard to raise awareness of the threat to the livelihood of the *corcheros*, a campaign which proved reasonably successful when many consumers refused to purchase bottles with plastic stoppers.

Cork is the outer layer of the trunk of the tree and is made up of a network of tiny watertight cells, which are filled with air and held together by a resinous substance. Cork oaks are very unusual because the tree can be stripped of 90 per cent of its bark and still survive — a practice that would kill many trees. Once the tree has been stripped it is more susceptible to injury until it grows a new protective layer. You can easily identify a cork oak that has had its bark harvested: the naked trunk is an eye-catching deep red.

Cork grows during the wet season and is ready for its first harvest when the tree is about 25 years old. The bark is cut back to the cambium layer, the layer in the trunk that generates new cell growth. The tree regenerates its bark so that it can be harvested every eight or nine years. Although this seems like a very long, slow process, each healthy tree produces several hundred kilos of cork at each harvesting and the trees live for many centuries. The largest cork oak in Portugal has produced 1,200 kilos (2600 lbs) in a single harvest. Harvesting is a skill which involves stripping away the bark in large pieces without damaging the tree, ensuring that the growing layer is left intact. Incisions are made in the bark, about one metre (3.3 ft) long and 30 centimetres (12in) across. The pieces are then gently prised away from the trunk with a special axe or curved saw, producing large rectangular "tiles" of cork which are stacked and allowed to season. Seasoning stabilises the cork and helps to keep the moisture content more uniform. The cork is then boiled in purified water, which softens it and extracts any chemicals. Once dry, the cork is graded. The first and second harvestings from a cork tree provide rough and uneven cork which is usually used for floors and insulation. Not until the third harvest is the cork considered of sufficiently good, smooth quality to be used for sealing bottles. It is amazing to think that the corks we so casually pull out of wine bottles have taken a tree at least 50 years to produce.

It was the monk Dom Perignon, allegedly the creator of champagne as we know it, who stimulated the commercial use of cork for wine bottles when he used it to seal his champagne bottles. Cork's suitability for plugging bottles lies in its ability to be compressed to half its size without losing any of its flexibility or expanding in another direction. Once corks have been pressed from the best quality bark, the remaining cork is amalgamated with that of inferior quality and used in an vast range of products. Cork is not only a brilliant insulator; it is also sound-proof and water-proof. We are all familiar with cork tiles, notice boards and gaskets for cars, but cork is also used in the production of fishing floats and buoys, dart boards, golf balls and for insulating pipes in meat production plants and cold storage units.

The holm oak, or *encina* (also known as the evergreen oak), looks very different to a cork oak. It grows wild throughout the Iberian peninsula and used to be one of the commonest trees, but large-scale felling for wood has considerably reduced its numbers. Its leaves resemble holly leaves, but the trees are easily identified as oaks by the long, thin acorns they produce in abundance. The threat of desertification through the Iberian peninsula has resulted in a programme of tree-planting and, in particular, the planting of holm oaks. The original programme aimed to reforest many areas with pine trees, because they are fast-growing, but the thick carpet of dried pine needles under the trees creates an increased fire risk. Project MedOak aims to plant oaks, because although they are slower growing than pines they are more fire resistant.

Spain and Portugal's oak forests are not only invaluable for their cork and the protection they offer wildlife. They are the main food source of the *pata negra*, the Iberian black-legged pig, which feeds on the acorns, or *bellotas*, produced by the oaks. Cured hams are an integral part of the cuisine of many Mediterranean countries. Italy has its Parma ham, France its *jambon cru* and Spain its *jamón serrano*. *Serrano* means "from the mountains" and refers to the place where the ham is cured, rather than where it comes from. If you have perused the vast range of hams for sale, you are probably curious about the difference in prices. Cured hams may all look very similar but some cost twice as much as others. The quality, and therefore the price, of mountain-cured ham depends on the breed of pig, its diet, the particular cut and the drying process. To cure the ham, joints of raw ham are covered with salt and left for a couple of weeks to draw out any excess moisture. Then the salt is washed off and the hams are hung to dry for about six months. Depending on the size and type of ham, as well as the weather conditions, the hams are then hung for a further six to 18 months to cure. This process takes place in mountain areas, where the drying sheds, or *secaderos*, are open to the cold mountain air which blows through and air-dries the hams.

The quality of the ham does not depend solely on the drying method and the cut but on the breed of pig and its diet. Native Iberian free-range pigs, which spend their lives grazing on acorns in the forests, provide the highest quality hams but, as this is a slow, expensive process, it accounts for only five per cent of total ham production. Most of the market is supplied by the more cost-effective White pig and the quality depends on the feeding-fattening process. Just as there are standards for olive oil and wine, there are standards for *jamón serrano*. The *Instituto Nacional de Denominaciones de Origen* regulates the establishment of denominated areas, the DO, as recognised ham-producing areas, such as Extremadura, Salamanca, Huelva or Teruel. The DO not only sets the standards but controls the whole process of production from pig to *jamón*. So the dilemma of knowing which *jamón* to purchase is really very simple: the price will reflect the quality and flavour.

Not content with being a major factor in the production of wonderful *jamón*, acorns are also the source of a rich, soothing liqueur called, simply, *bellota*. Try incorporating this nutty syrup into desserts such as ice-cream or poured over hot sponge puddings.

Oak forests have been so fundamental to the Iberian economy that the first laws protecting oak trees were brought in as early as 1320 by the Portuguese king, Dinis. Since the 1920s it has been illegal to cut down oak trees for any purpose other than essential thinning or to replace old trees. Oak trees are still protected in Spain and, if you wish to cut down an established tree, you must apply to the *Ministerio de Medio Ambiente* for permission.

Cultivation

Botanical names: cork oak - *Quercus suber holm oak* - *Quercus ilex*
A genus of over 600 species, some of which are evergreen. Oak trees produce separate male and female flowers on the same tree and are wind-pollinated. Male flowers are in the form of catkins while female flowers are often single flowers or small spikes. Their fruit, the acorn, is single-seeded. Oaks are drought-tolerant but like high rainfall in winter with well-drained soil.

Propagation

Oaks are easily propagated from acorns, so easily that we are continuously having to remove baby holm oaks from our garden or we would be overtaken by them. For propagating it is best to gather the acorns from the tree because those on the ground may already have been attacked by insects. Collect them in autumn. Discard any with holes in them. Plant the acorn, either on its side or point down, so that half of it is buried in the soil. Use good-quality soil that drains well. When the seedlings are 2cm (5in) tall, you can re-pot them or plant them in the ground.

Pruning

Prune in autumn. Oaks should not require any specific pruning, but cut away any dead or diseased wood.

Pests and Diseases

Oaks are frequently attacked by gall wasps and may suffer from fungal infections.

CHAPTER 9

OLIVES, part one

Tree: *olivo*
Olive: *aceituna*
Oil: *aceite de oliva*

If there is one tree that conjures up images of the Mediterranean, it is without doubt the olive. Ancient groves define the landscape throughout Italy, Greece, France and Spain, mile after mile of silver-leafed olive trees slumbering in the hot sun. During my first years in Andalusia I wandered around the groves, revelling in the twisted, gnarled trunks and loving the feeling of "foreign-ness" they embody, a feeling of warmth, sparkling light and the exotic. When the romantic phase gave way to the practical, we realised that we must do something with all these trees and threw ourselves on the mercy of our neighbour José. He began our initiation into the mysteries of olives by informing us that our groves contained at least seven different varieties. I gazed across the hills, speechless. All that I could see were rows of identical-looking trees.

I had heard of different varieties, the *kalamata* olives of Greece, for example, but I imagined that certain of them were specific to particular countries and was unaware that each country possessed many different varieties. Now better informed, I realise that I got away lightly with only seven varieties. In fact, more than 700 varieties of cultivated olive exist. I wasn't quite as naïve as many of our visitors who think olives are similar to grapes, either green or black. I knew that green olives ripened into black olives but, as I wandered around my land, all that I could think was that all the trees looked much the same and an olive was an olive was an

81

olive! After several years of harvesting and pruning, I can now recognise different varieties and know something about each fruit's attributes. Names such as *"picual"* and *"hojiblanca"* slide off the tongue like slippery olives and I can peruse supermarket shelves with some knowledge of the qualities of different oils and their applications.

In countries where olive trees grow in abundance the fruit and the oil have always been a fundamental part of life. Not only is olive oil the main source of income for most farmers but olives and oil are used extensively on a day-to-day basis, for cooking, baking, anointing bread, sprinkling over salads, as fuel for lamps, for moisturising skin and making soap. So crucial was the olive to life in ancient Greece that mythology suggests Zeus considered it more useful to mankind than the horse. In history and mythology these noble trees, reputed to grow up to a 1,000 years old, have represented strength, sacrifice and fertility, but most notably the olive branch symbolises peace. In ancient Greece the fruit of the tree was considered sacred — so much so that harvesting olives could only be undertaken by virgins or young men sworn to chastity. With criteria like that, one wonders whether they experienced any difficulties getting a workforce together.

However, olives haven't always had a good press. In the 1980s growing concern about a rise in heart disease and oil's effect on cholesterol levels provoked bad publicity for olive oil, and all other cooking oils and fats. Reduction in demand for oil caused a crisis in the countryside and many Spanish *fincas* were abandoned. Without the income from olives, farms became unsustainable. Meanwhile, Mediterranean people continued to consume gallons of olive oil and consistently registered exceptionally low levels of heart disease. The discovery that, unlike other oils, olive oil is mono-unsaturated and may help to lower cholesterol rather than increase it stimulated new interest in the product and demand has soared throughout the world. As well as its beneficial effects on the heart, olive oil is a good source of vitamin E, is effective in treating peptic ulcers and constipation and has a high level of antioxidants believed to assist the body in resisting cancer.

The history of olives stretches back to ancient times, as a discovery on the Greek island of Santorini has revealed. Fossilised olive leaves found there date back to 37,000 BC. During the 8th century BC olives were taken from Greece to Italy and developing trade routes carried them on to Spain and France. The Moors were such great olive-lovers that they planted trees prolifically throughout their conquered Spanish lands to ensure continuous supplies of oil. Today the Moorish legacy lives on in the Spanish words for olive, *aceituna*, and oil, *aceite*, from the Arabic *zitun* and *zit*.

Olive trees have long, productive lives. Many trees live several hundred years and still produce fruit. The species of cultivated olive now prolific throughout Europe is the *Olea europaea*, a member of the *Olaceae* family, which includes jasmine and lilac. Around the countryside you may be able to identify two other types of olive: the wild olive, which has narrower leaves than the cultivated variety and produces very small, worthless fruit, and a small bush that is only vaguely recognisable as a relative of the olive.

European oil-producing countries compete fiercely, each insisting that it holds the accolade for the best oil on the market. Italian oil is extremely well promoted throughout northern Europe and America, commanding prices up to three times those of other oils, but the Italians are reluctant to admit that a lot of the oil they bottle and label as Italian has actually been imported from Spain. In fact more than a quarter of the world's olive oil is produced in Spain and 75 per cent of Spain's oil comes from Andalusia.

Spain has more than five million acres of olive groves and 24 denominated regions for olive oil production. All regions aim to achieve the standard Denomination of Origin guarantee. Many people are confused about the variety of standards and their relevance to what is in the bottle. In fact, so great was the confusion that in 1959 an intergovernmental agency, the International Olive Oil Council, was established in Madrid to centralise and coordinate all aspects of olive oil production. Linked to the United Nations Economic and Social Council, it embraces a comprehensive range of activities including technology, research, production, funding and standards. Its power lies in the fact that it has 23 member states and its decisions are mandatory. So the standards are set and controlled, but what do they mean? As more than one consumer has queried: "It can be either a virgin or not. But how is it possible to be EXTRA virgin?"

Part of the answer lies in the production process. Oil was traditionally extracted from olives by crushing and pressing. The very first pressing, sometimes called "cold-pressed" olive oil, is the purest. Subsequent pressing of the olives involves the addition of hot water and/or chemicals to extract as much oil as possible, obviously reducing the purity of the oil, a case of quantity not quality. Nowadays major commercial olive mills use centrifugal force to extract olive oil, although heat is still introduced in the process to increase the quantity. If the temperature is maintained below a certain limit, the oil can be classified as cold-pressed.

The first pressing produces oil that contains the lowest level of fatty acids. To qualify as extra virgin oil, the level of acidity must be lower than 1 per cent. Virgin oil can have an acidity level up to 2 per cent and ordinary olive oils can have acid levels as high as 3.5 per cent. Any oil with an acidity level higher than 3.5 per cent is classified as lamp oil. However, it isn't only the acidity that determines the classification. A panel of tasters assess and grade olive oil for appearance, aroma and taste. Out of a possible 9 marks, oil must score higher than 6.5 to be classified as extra virgin.

Whether you are growing olives for oil, for eating, or purchasing it from a co-operative or supermarket, it helps to know something about the types of oil produced by different varieties and their qualities. Years ago I naively believed that all olive oil, apart from extra virgin, was pretty much the same. This is far from the case. The flavour of oil, as well as its level of acidity, bitterness, viscosity etc., determines whether it is more suitable for frying or dressing food. Differing climatic conditions and soil throughout Spain determine the type of olive tree most appropriate to the region, so that each area of the country produces an oil with very marked characteristics. There is just as much rivalry between the regions of Spain regarding the quality of their oil as there is between the oil-producing countries.

Numerous cookery programmes and books promote the health benefits of olive oil and encourage its use in place of other vegetable oils, butter, or margarine, but their main rule of thumb seems to be embodied in the phrase "use extra virgin for salad dressing and cheaper oils for cooking". This is helpful advice, but seems slightly basic when you are faced with a supermarket shelf stocked with several varieties of each of those oils. Without doubt, consumers are becoming better informed and are more likely to choose an appropriate oil. Individual taste has a lot to do with it. The best way through the maze is to try as many varieties as possible, but meanwhile I hope that the following brief summary of the main types of olives and oil produced in Spain may prove useful.

Málaga produces two of the best oils for culinary purposes: *hojiblanca* and *verdial*.

Hojiblanca for frying and baking. This olive grows well in soil with a high lime content and is principally found around Antequera and Córdoba. The oil has a high acid content, which makes it particularly suitable for deep frying. Its name "white leaves" refers to the underside of the leaves which are closer to white than the usual silver.

Verdial, native to the Axarquía (eastern part of Málaga province), particularly the Riogordo area, but also known as the *Verdial de Badaza y Extremadura*. This large olive is excellent as either a table olive or as salad dressing oil. It has a soft, fruity flavour which enhances the flavour of *gazpacho*.

Picural is the world's most important olive. Its name (from *pico*, Spanish for "beak") denotes the shape of the olive, but it has several other names such as *martena, loperana, temprana, corriente, morcana*. The trees dislike soil with a high lime content but are more frost resistant than most and grow well on high slopes. In Jaén province 97 per cent of olive trees are the *picural* variety. Their oil is good for general purposes, suitable for salad dressing, *gazpacho* and frying, but particularly good for stews and casseroles. Oil from *picural* olives is longer lasting than most and will keep for a couple of years if protected from heat and light.

Arbequina olives produce the oil preferred by gourmets and connoisseurs. It does not respond well to heat and should not be used for cooking, but it is considered superlative for dressing food. Unlike fine wines, it does not keep well and is best used when very young. Although traditionally grown in the Catalan region, *arbequina* trees are being increasingly planted in the province of Córdoba. The average production ratio of olives to oil is four kilos of olives per litre of oil, but 12 kilos of *arbequina* olives are required to produce one litre of oil.

Lechin olives are found throughout Andalusia but mostly in the province of Seville. It is a difficult oil to produce because the tree has a short flowering season and the flowers drop quickly, making the yield of fruit highly unpredictable. The oil is not as viscous as many olive oils and it is the most suitable oil for foods that are to be grilled.

Picudo is mainly grown in the Córdoba region but can be found throughout Andalusia. It is an extremely hardy, adaptable tree with dark, green leaves and very delicately flavoured olives suitable for eating either green or black. The oil, sweet and delicate without any hint of bitterness, is best for salads or drizzling on bread.

Olive oils do not improve with age and, generally speaking, the best flavour will be found in young oils. All olive oils are prone to oxidisation and should be stored in a dark place. After one year most oils will be edging towards rancid. There is just as much to learn about table olives. Many visitors imagine that they can pick an olive from the tree, pop it in the mouth and the flavour of the Mediterranean will burst the tongue. Despite telling them that this is not the case, even with ripe olives, most do not believe us and insist on trying the black, glistening fruit for themselves. It takes only a few seconds for the look of anticipation to give way to one of horror as bitterness fills their mouths. How the whole process of preparing olives for eating was ever discovered I cannot imagine, as it seems such an involved affair.

Your Spanish neighbours can advise you about curing your olives for eating, but almost every one will give you a different recipe. Morocco alone has over a hundred different recipes. Basically, green olives have to be cured for a few weeks to draw out the bitterness, after which you can store them with whatever additional flavours you wish to add, if any. Black olives are cured differently (see section on harvesting and curing for method and recipes).

Greece is one of the world's largest producers of plump, black table olives. Generally, the Spanish prefer green table olives to black and the *manzanilla* olive is one that you will frequently encounter (not to be confused with *té de manzanilla*, camomile tea). Often stuffed with anchovies or chillies, this is a very large, plump olive which is resistant to bruising and one of the first varieties that I managed to identify on our land. Up till then I simply thought that it had grown larger than the others because the growing conditions were exactly right for the tree and that, given the same treatment, all other olives would grow to the same size. The other well-known table olives are *gordal*, a medium large fruit which ripens early, and *sevillano* olives, which have a very low oil content and are only used for pickling. *Sevillano* is the olive frequently found in tins.

Two types of residue, one solid and one liquid, are left after olives have been processed several times and as much oil as possible has been extracted from them. The solid residue, *orujo*, was traditionally mixed with bran and fed to pigs. The liquid residue, *alpechin*, could be added to water and used as plant fertiliser. Until relatively recently, many mills simply discharged the residue directly into rivers, causing them to run black, or straight into fields in such quantities that it inhibited any plant growth. A legacy of this practice lives on in our area in a field of black sludge which emanates a very distinctive smell in the summer heat.

Residues are now frequently sold to producers of commercial fertilisers. Also experiments are under way to find ecological solutions for its disposal. Some success has been achieved with turning solid residue into bricks by mixing it with clay. An effective, slow-burning fuel has been made by compressing the residue under extremely heavy pressure to produce logs. In the United States olive stones have been crushed and mixed with bitumen to make road surfaces. Research continues and, who knows?, maybe one day we will drive our cars around the *campo* fuelled by the residue from olive oil production.

CHAPTER 10

OLIVES, part two; cultivation

Now you know something about the mysteries of this archetypal Mediterranean tree, the next step is to cultivate it and bring in that first harvest.

Botanical name: *Olea europaea*
The olive tree is native to the Mediterranean, Africa, Asia and Australasia. Height 6m (20ft) or more, although usually kept shorter for easy picking and pruning. Evergreen and hardy down to –8C. Fast-growing when young but slow-growing to maturity. Leaves 8cm (3in) long, grey-green above and silvery underneath. Insignificant small, yellow flowers appear in spring and give way to fruit which ripens in early autumn through to winter. Likes full sun, well-drained soil and does not require watering in summer once established.

PROPAGATION

Cuttings

Olive trees put out suckers from the bottom of each tree. You can simply cut these off and plant them or try propagating olive trees from the pruned stems of your existing tree. Use woody stems that are two to three years old, each about 2cm (3/4in) wide and 20cm (8-10in) long. Remove all the leaves and dig a trench a few centimetres deep and as long as the stem. Place the stem horizontally in the trench. Cover with earth, water and within a few months it should produce some lateral stems.

Seed

You can produce olives from the stones, but first you must remove the oil by soaking the stones in a lye (caustic soda)

solution and then store them in a dry place. During the summer crack the stones with a hammer and plant them. They should germinate in 40 to 50 days and will be ready for transplanting when they have grown six leaves. Trees propagated from seed are unlikely to be like the parent tree and may revert to the wild olive variety. Although the above methods of propagation can be fun to experiment with, they are rather hit-and-miss. By far the best and quickest way of establishing new trees on your land is to plant saplings. Olive trees of varying sizes can be purchased from most garden centres, reasonably priced and handy if you only require one or two trees. However, if you are thinking of bulk-buying, most towns and villages have a local supplier where you can purchase large quantities of young trees at a price competitive with those of the garden centres. Make sure you choose a variety suitable for your requirements. The supplier will be able to advise you which varieties grow best in your area.

Planting

For the best chance of success, plant trees between two and six years old, which will be more certain to take root and establish themselves quickly. They can be planted at any time of year but respond better to planting in late winter or early spring. Local people recommend digging a hole no less than one metre deep. If you are planting a lot of trees or a whole olive grove, it is faster and less strenuous to employ a mini-digger to dig all the holes. Olive trees are generally tolerant of wind but like well-drained soil.

Flowering

Olive flowers are so insignificant that many people are under the impression that the trees do not flower. Anyone who suffers from hay fever knows this is not the case and allergies to olive pollen are rife throughout the countryside. The tiny, creamy yellow flowers start to appear in February and are difficult to see among the leaves. Most people are first aware of the flowers when they see lots of tiny yellow particles blowing around their land. Olives have two types of flower: one containing both male and female parts and one with stamens only. Generally wind-pollinated, most olive trees will be self-pollinating, although there are some varieties that need other varieties nearby in order to set fruit.

Fertilising and after-care

Although olives need very little after-care, some fertilisation is beneficial two or three years after planting. The recommended fertiliser is urea. Local people remove weeds from around the trunk of the tree in late spring or early summer. You will often see a circle of bare soil around the tree trunks extending as wide as the overhanging branches. As well as letting the roots breathe, this acts as a fire break when weeds dry into scrub during the summer months and makes it much easier to gather the olives when harvesting begins. Although weed-clearing is often done by hand, some farmers employ tractors to pull tyres on chains over the land to drag the offending weeds up by the roots.

Pests and diseases

Chemical spraying is employed extensively to counter the numerous pests and diseases that affect olives. Pieces of plastic tied to trees to indicate where chemicals have been sprayed hang around the countryside for months like dirty pieces of washing caught in the branches. Some trees have red bags or pieces of material tied to them and some white. The colour does not bear any relation to the type of chemical sprayed and those marked with red have not been sprayed with anything more dangerous than those with white. During the years I have lived in Andalusia I have heard numerous theories expressed regarding the purpose of these markers, one being that trees with red plastic dangling from them have changed owners in a poker game. One school of thought suggests you will never be able to eliminate all pests and diseases from olive trees and some have to be tolerated. If the tree is well-looked after, i.e. all dead and diseased wood is pruned away allowing lots of sunlight to the branches and the soil around the base is aerated, the tree will be resistant to almost every predator and disease.

As education raises awareness among the farming community regarding the use of chemicals, moves increase to grow olives organically, but this can prove difficult if neighbours use chemicals which can blow or leak on to surrounding land and especially if they employ aerial spraying. For further information on pests and diseases and their treatment, refer to Chapter 18.

Pruning

Olives are easy trees to prune because they are very forgiving and will survive almost any abuse so, even if you are a complete novice, do not be frightened. It is virtually impossible to kill a tree. Even if it has been reduced to a stump, it is likely to regenerate and may even be healthier for it — and I speak from traumatic experience. My husband has a very good line in severe "creative" pruning, much to my initial horror when he reduced a whole grove of olives to stumps, one particular tree being left with only 12 leaves. Thankfully, the trees went on to flourish. There is no definitive way to prune but theories abound, one of the more prosaic being that trees should be cut back so that a swallow can fly through without touching the branches. This makes sense as it allows light through the trees and space for new growth. It's a good idea to cut away any dead wood and keep the tree fairly low-growing so that you don't have to climb high to access the olives.

Mistletoe

One problem that can prove persistent and irritating if you have a neighbour who does not maintain his trees is mistletoe. That romantic sprig of greenery with its pretty white berries that you pay a fortune for at Christmas in your home country can be a real pest. Mistletoe is a parasitic plant with extremely sticky berries which are very attractive to birds. The birds digest the berries and then excrete the seeds onto the branches of neighbouring trees where the plant spreads rapidly. Once mistletoe has established itself on a branch, it develops a root system which penetrates into the water-conducting area of the tree, depriving it of both water and nutrients. Left unchecked, an invasion of mistletoe will eventually kill the tree. Once it has started growing on a branch, the only effective way to deal with it is to prune it out as quickly as possible, which can often mean removing a complete limb. This can be a nightmare if, as in our case, you have a neighbour who does not look after his trees and has allowed mistletoe to become established, because there is no way of stopping it spreading. Apart from offering to prune your neighbours' trees, you have to be ever-watchful and keep pruning away limbs of your own trees.

If you do nothing else to your trees, please be thoughtful about your neighbours and their livelihood. If you spot mistletoe growing on your trees, prune it all away before it gets out of control. Prune tree any time from November through to early spring after the olives have been harvested. Many locals tend to harvest and prune the tree at the same time, using a wide range of implements from long-handled pruning saws to chainsaws. Chainsaws, which substantially reduce pruning time, are becoming the preferred tool for the job and the sight of our neighbour leaping along branches wielding a chain saw fills me with awe and trepidation. The invention of chainsaws with long handles removes the risks involved in climbing into trees with a lethal tool, a great bonus, preserving life and limb. Apart from cutting off a few limbs, you need to saw all the branches into logs for transporting out of the fields. Olive trees generally have a variable rate of fruit production and produce well in alternate years so, if you have pruned your tree and the harvest is poor the following year, don't panic. It is the nature of the tree not your slash-and-burn technique.

Harvesting

Harvest time is signalled by the olives ripening and falling to the ground but also by a sudden burst of activity in the *campo*.

Babbles of conversation fill the air, sticks bang rhythmically against branches, numerous three-wheelers chug noisily along tracks and braying mules patiently wait to be laden with sacks full of glistening olives. In Andalusia, the picking season usually starts in early November, while further north it can be as late as January.

In autumn you may see women scrabbling about on the ground with baskets and buckets collecting the olives that have already dropped. This is a slow painful process, heavy on the back and knees and not particularly wonderful for the fingers, although the oil encountered in the fruit does make your nails and the skin on your hands beautifully glossy. The first year I harvested olives I spent hours meticulously picking fruit from the ground. It seemed to take forever to fill a sack. I proudly took it along to my neighbours who were willing to incorporate our olives with theirs for oil production. They inspected the contents of my sack to ensure that I hadn't included too many twigs etc. and then looked at me in amazement.

"Are these for eating or oil?" they asked.

"Oil, of course. That was the arrangement," I replied.

They delved deeper into the sack and then exclaimed: "But each one is perfect!"

In my enthusiasm to do everything correctly and make sure that I did not contaminate the resulting oil in any way I had meticulously scrutinised every single olive and discarded any that were damaged, flawed, nibbled or slightly rotten. No wonder it took me so long to gather a sack full. My neighbours thought it highly amusing and it was worth the hours of work to witness the depth of their chuckles. However, since then I have discovered that some olive mills set very high standards and insist that olives gathered from the ground (damage to the fruit triggers acidity) are milled separately from those picked from the tree, which produce better-quality oil with lower acidity levels.

Throughout Spain olives are still predominantly harvested by hand. A couple of large nets (*mantas*) are spread on the ground under the tree and the tree is bashed with a long stick (*vara*) until all the olives have dropped on to the net. They are then separated from the leaves and twigs and sacked for transport to the mills. Nets, sticks and pruning saws can be purchased from local ironmongers or agricultural suppliers. In areas of large-scale production, olives are harvested mechanically. You will see machines shaking the olives loose by gripping the tree trunks and rhythmically vibrating them. Some believe that banging the tree with a pole damages the new branches, others say that using machines damages the roots. Enthusiastic oil producers who insist on the highest standards throughout their oil production spurn both methods and will only consider harvesting olives manually. Stripping the branches by hand is best undertaken when the olives have just turned black but are still firm. Sliding a hand down along the branch with a gentle stroking action will loosen the fruit without damaging it. This method produces the purest olive oil as it minimises bruising to the fruit, which tends to trigger acidity. A recent innovation, available from some agricultural suppliers, is a plastic rake which is used to strip olives from the branches.

What to to with your olives

Once your olives have been harvested and sacked, you must do something with them fairly rapidly. The fermentation process begins quickly and the olives will soon rot, becoming acidic and mouldy. They must be converted to oil within a few days of being picked, hence the long rows of vehicles queuing outside olive mills late into the night. Converting olives into oil is a lengthy, time-consuming process, involving a lot of equipment which makes it difficult, but not impossible, to do on a small scale. If you have many trees, you may wish to attempt it as a cottage industry but bear in mind the time constraints between harvesting and milling, plus the amount of labour involved in both.

Do you simply want to sell your olives for cash or do you want to receive the equivalent in olive oil? Even if you only have a few sacks of olives, you can take them direct to the olive mill, or *fábrica de aceite*. Many mills are willing to accept even one sack of your produce, but as you may have a long wait for your sack to be weighed it can be easier to amalgamate your crop with a neighbour's. The oil you receive from the mill will be a mix of all the olives milled. If you have been growing your olives organically or you want oil that is specific to your crop, you must find a producer willing to do a run solely for your delivery. Some commercial mills will accept 600 kilos (1,320lbs) of olives for a specific pressing, but there are few of these left. Various private mills dotted around will accept amounts as small as 150 kilos (330lbs). They charge a small amount (currently about 12 euros per 50 kilos, or 110 lbs) to undertake the milling. As the minimum weight of olives accepted and the amount charged vary from mill to mill, it is worth spending time researching your local mills before harvesting because once your olives are in sacks you have to act quickly.

If you wish to sell your olives, you can go direct to the *fábrica* and elect to receive cash instead of oil. As an alternative, some areas are serviced by olive collectors with large flatbed trucks equipped with weighing scales. They usually collect at least twice a week and pay cash-in-hand. The payment is per kilo and varies considerably, not just from year to year but from week to week.

Olive oil cooperatives

Spain has an excellent history of cooperatives and most areas have several producing olive oil. Membership lies with the land, not with the owner. Thus, if you have purchased land whose previous owner was a member of the cooperative, you can exercise your rights as a member even if you are an *extranjero*. If you do not know whether the previous owner was a member, your neighbours probably will, or you can take the *plan catastral* of your land along to the cooperative and they will check for you. If your land is involved with the coop and you wish to take advantage of the grants available, you must register with them by mid-October. Requirements can change from year to year, but usually you require your *residencia* or NIE and a bank certificate with details of your account so that the co-operative can pay in any money you're entitled to. The cooperative will organise all the relevant forms for you and each time you take your olives for milling the weight will be recorded. Any money and subsidies owing to you will be paid at the end of the season, or a few months later.

Harvesting and curing green table olives

Pick your olives from the tree when they have reached their maximum size and before they begin to turn purple. There are two main ways to treat the olives, with lye (caustic soda) or water.

Water method: Once they have picked their olives, country folk bash the olives with a stone to break the skin, which allows water to penetrate the flesh of the fruit and draw out the bitterness. There is a knack to hitting hard enough to break the skin without completely crushing the olive. Spanish tradition says that olives should not be cut with anything metal and, once the skin is broken, they should not be touched with anything metal. In Morocco, however, olives are slit with knives and I have saved a lot of time cutting mine with a knife without experiencing any problems with the resulting olives. Cover the bashed (or slit) olives completely with cold water. At this stage you can add a small amount of salt to the water — this seems to be a matter of personal taste. Change the water every two or three days. The time that the olives should be soaked varies. Some people recommend six to eight days, others say a month, another matter of personal taste. The best test: sample them after a week and see what you think. Once ready for eating, your olives can be stored in salt water, vinegar or olive oil, but you can have fun experimenting with different seasonings and marinades. The more usual additions to olives are sliced peppers, chilli peppers, herbs, anchovies, cloves of garlic, peppercorns and lemon. Try a marinade mixing ingredients to taste or try one of the recipes at the end of the chapter.

Curing with lye: If you prefer your olives unbroken, you must cure them with lye, known as *cáustico* and sold in *droguerias*. Place the olives in a large container of stoneware, ceramic or glass. Add one tablespoon of lye to each litre of water. N.B.: always add the crystals to the water and not the water to the crystals, to prevent splashing the chemical. Pour the solution over the olives, making sure they are covered. Place a saucer or plate on top to submerge all the olives. Cover the jar and leave for 12 hours. Drain the olives, make a new batch of lye solution and repeat the process. After a further 12 hours, test one of the olives to see if the lye has penetrated. If they are ready, the olives will be easy to cut and soft through to the middle. If they are not ready, soak them in a fresh batch of lye solution for another 12 hours. Rinse the olives and soak them in fresh water for two to three days, changing the water several times a day. Taste the olives and when they suit your palate place them in a solution of salt water (one large tablespoon of salt per litre of water). The olives will now be ready for eating or marinading. Warning : remember that lye is caustic. Always wear rubber gloves and do not use any plastic containers or utensils.

Marinades for green olives

juice and zest of two lemons
1/2 tsp paprika
1/2 tsp cumin
1 tbsp of good olive oil

Toss all the ingredients together and pour over cured olives. They will be ready to eat after a couple of days.

75g (2.5oz) salt
100ml (4floz) white wine vinegar
600ml (22floz) water
1/2 orange
1 bay leaf
3 tbsp oregano

Mix all the ingredients together, add a kilo of olives and marinade for eight days.

Curing black olives: Some people cure black olives in salt water, but I have not had much success with this method. The colour bled from the olives and they looked unappetising. The best method seems to be dry-curing them in salt. Prick the olives all over with a pin or fork and layer them with rock salt, about 110 grams of salt per kilo of olives. Toss them whenever the mood takes you and they should be ready for eating in one week. If you want your olives in a hurry, try the Provencal method of freezing them for a day, which reduces the curing time by a third. In France many people do not harvest their table olives until after the first frost to reduce the time involved in the curing process.

CHAPTER 11
POMEGRANATES

Pomegranate: *granada*

Pomegranates are either loved for their fresh juicy taste or hated for the vast number of seeds that stick between the teeth. The name is a very apt fusion of *pomme* (apple) and *granat* (many-seeded). The peculiarity of the pomegranate makes it a difficult fruit to ignore and throughout history it has been credited with mystical properties.

Cultivated since ancient times, the pomegranate is defined in Arabic mythology as the apple presented by Eve to Adam. In Judaism the pomegranate is a symbol of fertility, its many seeds encapsulating the commandment "be fruitful and multiply". However, in Greek mythology it is the fruit responsible for determining the seasons. When Persephone, the daughter of Demeter (the goddess of nature), was abducted by Pluto and taken to the underworld, Demeter grieved and threw the world into permanent winter. When Demeter appealed to Zeus to intercede and return her daughter, Zeus complied but imposed the strange constraint that Persephone could only return to her mother if she had not eaten any food during her captive period. The poor girl had chewed six pomegranate seeds to help quench her thirst, not unreasonable you may think when you've been abducted to Hades. The unforgiving Zeus decreed that Persephone must spend six months on earth during which time her mother is happy, summer arrives and everything blossoms, then six months back in Hades, her punishment for each pomegranate seed. Demeter grieves during the six months apart from her daughter and brings winter upon us.

Pomegranates are deciduous trees and, in keeping with their role of bringing six months of winter upon the earth, their leaves disappear early and, compared with other Mediterranean trees, their flowers are late arriving. In a country where most trees are evergreen, pomegranates provoke a pang of nostalgia in autumn when their leaves turn from green to vivid gold, but then we pay the price with only dark, gloomy branches to look at for the next four or five months. They don't show much greenery before the end of February and are slow to come into full leaf, though well worth waiting for. The beautiful orange-red flowers which follow in April and May are strong in colour and very waxy in texture. In fact, pomegranate flowers look and feel so much like wax flowers that it is difficult to believe they are real. They cling tenaciously to the stems of the tree for several weeks before developing quickly into fruit. Once the fruit has ripened, pomegranates have the extremely irritating habit of bursting open on the tree, so — if you want to harvest them before they split — watch them carefully and leap into action at just the right moment. But be careful where you leap: some of the branches have large, painful thorns.

The pomegranate is the symbolic fruit of Spain and nowhere is this more evident than in Granada where fruit and city share the name. The famous Alhambra palace built by the Moors has a whole gateway dedicated to their beloved pomegranate and the fruit is included in the city's coat of arms. Incongruously, considering the romantic associations, a *"granada"* in Spanish also signifies "hand grenade", apparently because they are similar in size and shape to pomegranates and tend to shatter into many small pieces.

Pomegranate seeds are used in many Turkish, Arabic and Indian dishes to provide a slightly acidic note. Pomegranate juice is tart and has been compared to the taste of unripe raspberries, thus the juice, seeds and pulp were desirable culinary ingredients in a world where the more acidic lemon had not yet revealed itself. The seeds are usually dried and ground before being added to sauces and provide an alternative to mango powder, lemon, or lime juice. Two teaspoons of ground pomegranate seeds are roughly equivalent to one teaspoon of lemon juice. Pomegranate juice provided the base for grenadine syrup, well-loved in France. Grenadine is now made with synthetic colouring and flavouring, so if you have some pomegranate trees try producing your own syrup. It is easy to produce and will be far superior to anything you can buy.

Not only the fruit of the pomegranate tree has been utilised throughout the world. In Africa the bark, roots and the rind of the fruit provide tannin and dye for treating leather, particularly Morrocan leather. Pomegranate bark was also used in the treatment of fevers. Farmers cut the straightest suckers from the pomegranate and dry them to make handles for tools. Nicholas Culpepper, the 17th-century English herbalist, described the flowers and bark of pomegranate as "astringent", particularly effective in stemming bleeding. He recommended an infusion of the fruit to cure ulcers of the mouth and throat and to "fasten teeth", so if yours are feeling a little wobbly a glass of pomegranate juice can't go amiss.

Cultivation

Botanical name: *Punica granatum*
A deciduous, shrubby tree which will reach 4.5m (14.5ft) high and grows almost as wide. It has thin, twisting stems and long, sharp thorns. Pomegranate trees can grow in soil, with a high level of alkalinity that would kill most plants. They grow wild and prolifically in places where there is a natural source of water and make good hedges as well as ornamental container plants.

Flowers

Reddish orange-coloured, bell-shaped flowers with a waxy appearance and texture appear in late spring, either singly or in clusters at the end of branches. They cling tenaciously to the branches for several weeks, developing quickly into fruit.

Fruit

The tree must be grown in full sun for the fruit to ripen and, although it is drought-tolerant, it will fruit better if it finds or receives water. Humidity has a detrimental effect on the formation and low temperatures adversely affect the quality. Fruit develop during the summer up to 13cm (5in) in diameter and ripen quickly with a tendency to split once ripe. If they are not removed from the trees, the fruit will blacken and remain clinging to the branches throughout the winter. Small, immature fruit tend to dry on the stem and can be cut and used to good effect in floral decorations.

Pruning

Prune in autumn after the leaves have fallen and wear sturdy gardening gloves against those sharp thorns. Pomegranates can be kept low-growing to create hedges. Remove any suckers from the base of the tree.

Propagation

Although fairly long-lived, pomegranates' fruit production tends to decline after 15 years so it is a good idea to continuously propagate them. They can be grown from seed but greater success is likely to be achieved with cuttings. Cuttings root so easily that a friend ended up with a whole hedge of pomegranates when he pushed some prunings into the ground to hold an irrigation tube in place because each pruning quickly developed into a bush. Take cuttings in winter from branches that are at least one year old. Cut 26-30cm (10-12 in) lengths and remove the leaves. Plant them either in pots or straight into the ground to a depth of two-thirds of the cutting and keep moist.

Uses

Pomegranates were the original base of grenadine syrup, which is an excellent sauce for sponge pudding or ice cream and can be thinned to make a refreshing summer drink (see recipe at end of chapter). The seeds are still used in Indian and Arabic cooking.The flowers and bark are astringent and in mediaeval times were used to stop bleeding. An infusion of the fruit cures ulcers of the mouth and throat. Chickens love pomegranates. Split the fruit open and chickens dive on them with enthusiasm.

RECIPES

Pomegranate syrup

This recipe makes a delicious sauce for ice cream or desserts. Thinned with water (or gin if you prefer), it also makes a refreshing drink.

2kg (4lb) red pomegranates
400g (13oz) preserving or granulated sugar
few drops of lemon juice

Cut the pomegranates in half and extract all the juice (easily done with a juicer or a lemon squeezer). Filter the juice through muslin into a pan, add the sugar and lemon. Bring slowly to the boil. Keep stirring until the sugar has dissolved. Cook over a medium heat for 10-20 minutes until it becomes a clear light syrup. Remove from the heat. Skim across the top of the syrup and then pour it into clean, sterilised jars or bottles. The syrup keeps well when refrigerated. It freezes well and can be turned into a very refreshing water ice or sorbet.

Pomegranate seed and yoghurt marinade

In India pomegranate seeds, called *anardana*, are used for flavouring many dishes as well as breads such as *nan*. This marinade is perfect for chicken or lamb that is being prepared for barbecuing and has the added advantage of using up some of your extensive almond crop.

1cm piece cinnamon stick
1 tspn coriander seeds
1/2 tspn cumin seeds
1 cardamom pod
3 cloves
1 tablespoon almonds
1/2 tspn salt
4 garlic cloves crushed
2 tablespoons dried, ground pomegranate seeds
150 ml Greek-style yoghurt
1-2 tspn cayenne pepper.

Toast cinnamon and coriander over medium heat until they change colour. Add cumin, cardamom, cloves, and almonds, and roast until the cloves become puffy. Grind the spices with salt and add to all the other ingredients. Marinade meat for at least two hours and grill or barbecue.

CHAPTER 12

PRICKLY PEAR

Plant: *chumbera*
Fruit: *chumbo*

Also called the Indian or Barbary fig, the prickly pear cactus conjures up images of Mexico, that old stereotype of a figure wearing a large sombrero and brightly coloured *poncho* with cacti in the background. Evocative though the prickly pear may be of deserts and old cowboy films, it is also common in Andalusia, growing like a weed. Once established, if left to their own devices, these cacti spread over hillsides, forming impenetrable barriers difficult to remove. In Australia, South Africa and southern India they have become such a pest that the governments have taken action to control their spread and some countries have introduced the cactus pest *Cactoblastis cactorum* from Mexico. The caterpillars of this moth are voracious feeders and can speedily decimate prickly pear plantations, but the caterpillars attract their own predators, creating other environmental problems.

Prickly pears look exotic, especially when fruiting. Their orange-red fruit look quite appetising but, if you approach the plant, a puff of wind can blow small spiky hairs on to your skin and clothing, creating an irritation that will last for days. So fine are these hairs that they are almost impossible to get rid of. The only effective method I've discovered is to cover the afflicted area with sticky tape which, with luck, will pull out some of the hairs when it is stripped off. When you eventually manage to fight your way through the spiny pads and reach the fruit, you discover that it too is covered in spikes, called glochids. These will murder your hands and heaven forbid that you should get any of them in your gums.

Believe me, it's a good way of dieting because you will be unable to eat anything for days. By now you may have the impression that I am not over-keen on these particular exotic plants.

Prickly pears are of the genus *Opuntias (family Cactaceae)*, of which about 30 varieties are cultivated for their produce, plants with evocative names such as "hedgehog prickly pear", "bearded prickly pear" and "beavertail cactus". The variety that grows on Andalusian hillsides is usually *Opuntia ficus-indica*, brought here from Mexico. Tall with pads of leaves whose profile resembles Mickey Mouse ears, these exotic cacti flower in late spring and produce fruits similar in shape to figs, hence the name.

In its native Mexico and parts of the USA, the prickly pear is a delicacy known as "confectionery of the desert". Both the pads and the fruit are eaten either in their natural state or as jams and preserves. Street traders sell slices of candied cactus, cactus boiled in cane sugar, and the plant is also a source of both low-alcohol and alcoholic beverages. In Mexico the pads of the *Opuntia* are called *nopalito* and the fruits *tuna*, so if you see a Mexican recipe for "tuna" do not reach for a tin of fish.

In many desert or arid areas prickly pears are almost the only plants providing edible fruit and one can see its value in such a situation. But why would anyone want to introduce a fast-growing, thorny, prickly weed to Spain where fruit grows abundantly? The answer lies in dyes. *Opuntia ficus-indica* and *Opuntia coccinellifera* are both host plants to a scarlet insect that is the source of cochineal, a bright red dye used extensively in Mexico at the time of the Spanish conquest. Once the relationship between prickly pears, cochineal beetles and the vivid red dye was established, the conquistadors wasted no time exporting *Opuntia* to Spain and plantations were established to provide breeding grounds for the beetles. Because of its strong colour, the demand for cochineal dye grew and it was used extensively in the clothing, food and cosmetic industry. This dye produced the vivid, red colours of military jackets and — disgusting though the thought of smearing crushed beetles on your lips may seem — bright red lipstick was originally manufactured from cochineal. Cochineal has largely been replaced by synthetic dyes and demand for the beetles has diminished, but we are left with an extensive prickly legacy.

Ficus indica is not in great demand by the food industry in Europe. Market stalls or street-traders occasionally have odd boxes of prickly pears, but they are not sold on any large commercial scale. However, this may change because recent studies into *Opuntia* have revealed prickly pear to be a potentially valuable health food. The type of pectin contained in the fruit helps lower levels of "bad" cholesterol, the fruit and the pads have high levels of soluble fibre which help stabilise blood sugar, and research suggests the fruit could contribute to lowering the level of insulin required by diabetics. That barrier of thorny weeds marching its way down your land may well prove to be the cash crop of the future.

Many *campesinos* enjoy prickly pears and can be seen risking life and limb to pick the fruit. They are usually armed with a bucket and a staff of split cane which they use like tongs to grab the fruit and lift it clean away from the plant. Prickly pears are not just a source of food in the countryside, as their extremely fibrous pads are also hand-woven into rope.

Dense and fast-growing, quickly reaching heights useful for privacy, these cacti form good hedges. Their size and multitudinous spikes make them fairly impenetrable and the pads are full of moisture so they provide a good firebreak. However, they need to be kept well under control. They spread along untended land at an alarming rate as any pad touching or falling to earth roots and creates another plant. An added disadvantage is that the large amount of inaccessible fruit lying in the middle of the thicket attracts rats. Having battled with prickly pears for many years, I can't help thinking that they are more trouble than they are worth. Even if I was totally in love with the multi-seeded, melon-flavoured fruit, I would prefer to buy it from my neighbours or the market traders, who deserve to receive a ridiculously high return for picking and preparing this difficult fruit.

Cultivation

Botanical name: *Opuntia ficus indica*
A large evergreen plant with pads covered in spikes or glochids. Height 4metres (13ft); Width 4 metres (13ft). Flowers in late spring to early summer. Yellow flowers grow directly on the pads.

Propagation

Not a problem with prickly pear. Just lay one of the pads on the ground and it will root and, before you know it, you will have a hillside full of them. If you want them to root quickly, bury about 2cm (1in) of the pad in well-drained soil. They grow best in sunny positions and will grow in stony soil. Their ability to store water means that they are drought-resistant. They dislike moist, shady conditions.

Pruning

First get a pair of thick gardening gloves! I have found the best way to prune prickly pears is with a pruning saw on a very long handle so that I can stand as far away as possible. Never attempt it on a windy day because the hairs will blow on to your skin and clothes and irritate you for days. The moist, fibrous pads are easy to cut through, the easiest place being the narrow joint between each pad. The pads are so heavy that a hard blow is enough to dislodge them from the main plant. Old woody stems are fairly easy to saw through and are fascinating to look at, a wonderful weave of mesh-like fibres.

Prickly pears are almost indestructible and can be pruned at any time of year without really damaging the main plant, but if you want to stimulate a good crop to harvest prune them in late autumn or winter, after harvesting and before flowering. A neighbouring goat-herder can minimise pruning by leading his goats past your prickly pears. Goats feast on the whole plant, undeterred by thorny spines. Once you have reduced the plant to the size you want, what on earth do you do with the prunings? Moist and difficult to burn, they seem impossible to get rid of. If you leave them on the ground, the pads will start to root, but with all those prickles you don't want to transport them too far. We have found the best way to deal with them is to throw the pads back into the centre of the thicket where they rot down on top of one another (alternative suggestions welcome, on a post card please). Using good gloves, you can pick the pads up. Grab them at their base where there are fewest spines.

Harvesting

Fruit will ripen throughout the summer. As ripe fruit are very soft and difficult to gather, it is easiest to harvest them when they are still slightly firm. Ideally, pick them when they are starting to turn from green to yellow/red. A pair of long-handled barbecue tongs can prove useful.

Uses

The easiest way to eat the pears is to spear them with a fork, slice a piece off each end, slit along the fruit and peel the skin away or scoop the fruit out with a spoon. Do not touch the peel with your hands. The fruit taste rather like melon and have lots of seeds, which are edible when fresh but harden when stored. Puréed and sieved, the fruit makes a good accompaniment to ice-cream, or try making marmalade using any standard recipe for marmalade and the following quantities:

RECIPE

Prickly pear marmalade

  2 cups of pulp
  1/2 cup orange juice
  1 tablespoon lemon juice
  1 cup sugar
  strips of orange peel boiled for a few minutes in water

CHAPTER 13
AGAVE

Agaves are extremely distinctive plants frequently seen growing along the edges of fields. They're attractive — and fairly lethal. Each of the large, grey-green, leathery leaves, spear-shaped and growing in a rosette formation, is edged on both sides with evil-looking spikes which are particularly dangerous for children. When they are small, agaves look like interesting sculptural plants to edge a field or driveway. Beware! A quick glance around the landscape will reveal the monstrous size agaves can grow to, often reaching widths of 4 metres (13ft) and heights of 2 metres (6.6 ft).

The most common agave seen in Spain is the *Agave americana*, also known as the century plant because it was believed to flower every 100 years. In fact, it flowers from 10 years of age onwards, depending on growing conditions, but only once in its lifetime. The flowers are unbelievable: a single long shoot, bearing a distinct resemblance to giant asparagus, sprouts from the centre of the rosette in early summer and grows at a speed that is almost visible. This flower stalk grows about 30cms (1ft) each day to as high as 10 metres (33ft). The stalk then produces yellow flowers on alternate sides at the top of the stem and, once it has flowered and seeded, the main plant dies. The agave's tall flowers are not only surprising in their height, speed of growth and unusual shape but in that, in its native Mexico, they are pollinated by bats. By the time it has flowered and died, the agave will have a cluster of plantlets around its base which repeat the growth cycle. A variegated form of *Agave americana* seen around the Spanish countryside is the *Agave americana marginata*. Its distinctive leaves are similar in shape to the *Agave americana* and also spiky-edged, but they are bordered by a golden yellow stripe, giving the plant a much lighter appearance than the *americana*.

Mexico has 136 different species of native agave. The plants provide a valuable source of food and drink and are believed to have been cultivated for at least 9000 years. Drought-resistant, they are invaluable in dry areas, providing products which fulfil many human and animal needs. The tough fibrous leaves are the raw material for many useful items. From them the Aztecs manufactured paper similar in texture to papyrus; dried leaves were ground and smoked; the coarse fibres were pulped to make cloth, provided thread and twisted into rope. The *Agave sisalana* is the main source of sisal, originally used for rope but nowadays in great demand for carpets and mats. The lethal spikes on agave leaves were transformed into needles and pins and an extract from the leaves was compressed into a firm substance which reacts, and is used, in the same way as soap. Once all the leaves were removed from the plant, the heart and bulb of the plant, which are high in saccharine, were cooked and provided food for both humans and animals. The large flower stems were dried and used in building, especially for roofing where they provided strong water-proof thatch. The agave is a truly versatile and useful fast-growing plant.

Today the agave is particularly famous for those well- known spirits mescal and tequila. For centuries in South America Aztecs and native Indians have produced a variety of drinks from both the flower and the hearts of differing species of agave, the resulting liquor known locally as *sotal*, *bacanora* and *pulque*. Sweet sap can be extracted simply by slitting growing stems stem and tying a cup below the slit to gather the liquid, which is either drunk in its natural state or fermented. For large-scale production, the mature plants are roasted in charcoal pits, covered with strong fibrous mats and earth, to extract the sap. The resulting liquid was simply fermented and drunk until the arrival of the Spanish conquistadors who introduced the distilling process to produce the spirit known as mescal. During the 19th century mescal production matured into the more widely known drink tequila, named after the first town to refine the spirit, and more than 19 million gallons of this spirit are now produced each year, predominantly for export. Although all tequilas were originally mescals, nowadays the two drinks have characters as different as those of Scotch and Irish whisky. The use of differing varieties of agave, production methods and storage impart a flavour to tequila which many Mexicans believe has lost the taste and character of the original agave drink.

Whereas mescal is still produced from a variety of agaves, tequila is produced exclusively from the blue *Agave tequilana weber azul*. Once the plant is harvested, tequila is produced by baking or steaming the agaves and the sap distilled two or sometimes three times. Different flavours of tequila are developed by aging the spirit in oak barrels for up to four years. Tequila and mescal production are legally regulated. To control mescal quality and protect the name, the Mexican government passed laws in 1994 which limited legal production to six areas around the town of Oaxaca. About 100 million agave plants flourish on 40,000 hectares of legal plantations in Mexico, which must be an awesome sight. Meanwhile, many Mexicans continue to harvest agaves and produce pulque or mescal illegally. Bootleg liquor is produced in such large quantities that there are growing fears wild agaves will be over-harvested.

Cultivation

Botanical name: *Agave americana*
Height: 2m (6.6ft). Width: 4m (13ft).

Flowers

After 10 years' growth a single stem rises from the centre of the plant and produces yellow flowers on alternate sides of the stem. The plant starts flowering in early summer and the stem can reach a height of 10 meters (33ft). Once it has flowered the main plant dies.

Propagation

Agaves have to be one of the easiest plants to propagate. Simply dig up one of the small offshoots that grow around the base of the plant and plant it. They do not seem particularly fussy about soil or growing conditions but, once established, do not like too much water. If you are growing agaves close to a track, it is advisable to clip the lethal spikes off the side of each leaf with a pair of secateurs.

CHAPTER 14

ROSEMARY AND LAVENDER

Rosemary: *romero*

This highly aromatic shrub, native to the Mediterranean, grows wild and prolifically around the Spanish countryside. Its Latin name *Rosemarinus* stems from *Ros Marinus* meaning "dew of the sea". Legend has it that rosemary bushes produced only white flowers until the Virgin Mary, on her journey to Bethlehem, spread her blue cloak to dry over a rosemary bush. The colour from her cloak bled into the flowers changing them from white to blue. Spreading clothes over rosemary bushes isn't uncommon in the Mediterranean, particularly in Greece where many women prefer drying their washing this way because the wonderful fragrance permeates the cloth.

The Spanish name for rosemary, *romero*, is also the word for pilgrim, but Christianity is not the only religion that has associations with rosemary. The ancient Egyptians added rosemary to water for ritual cleansing and it was utilised across the spectrum of religious ceremonies from weddings to funerals. In ancient Greece rosemary symbolised both love and death and was burnt as incense in shrines. In western Europe rosemary was considered a sacred herb and bunches were hung outside houses to ward off evil spirits. Today, walking through Spanish cities you may encounter gypsy women handing out sprigs of rosemary to protect you and keep the evil spirits at bay, for a small "donation", of course.

In the Middle Ages rosemary was burned during exorcisms to smoke out devils. Now that we know more about the chemical properties of the herb, its reputation for repelling malign spirits seems justified. For western Europeans, burning rosemary produced the same result as the Aborigines burning

eucalyptus — the smoke contains strong antiseptic properties that help keep bugs at bay and slow the spread of disease. In fact, there are many similarities between eucalyptus and rosemary. Essential oils from both contain camphene and pinene, and both are antiseptic, useful in controlling the spread of disease and in treating respiratory problems. Just as the Aborigines smoked eucalyptus leaves so Nicholas Culpepper, the 17th-century herbalist, recommended shredding dried rosemary leaves and "smoking them as tobacco for coughs and consumption". Culpepper prescribed decoctions of rosemary for numerous complaints. But he does warn that it is good for "windiness in the stomach, bowels and spleen and expels it powerfully", so use it carefully or you may become anti–social.

In the culinary field, rosemary is frequently included in meat recipes, particularly with lamb, but this traditional marriage is not just about flavour. Wrapping meat with sprigs of rosemary retards the process of decay and is an effective method of preserving meat. Most of us have fridges and freezers to preserve our meat so these days we are unlikely to need to wrap it in herbs, but adding rosemary to roasting meat can be beneficial because we now know that the herb assists in reducing cholesterol.

Rosemary was one of the first herbs to be used in medicine and continued to be burned to fumigate some French hospital wards until the 20th century. In France it is called *incensier* and was traditionally sold in chemists for a wide range of complaints. Recommended for numerous ailments from hangovers to headaches, it was also believed that rosemary could restore hair and youth. Interestingly, research has now proven that rosemary is a beneficial herb in medical conditions where there is a reduction or loss of mental function. It has a stimulating effect on the brain and nervous system, increases mental clarity and is believed to assist in conditions where the patient has suffered loss of sense of smell or memory, reflected in Ophelia's well-known line in Hamlet "there's rosemary, that's for remembrance". Generally, rosemary has a stimulating effect on both the mind and body and its uplifting properties resulted in its inclusion in the original recipe for eau-de-cologne, or the "Queen of Hungary's Water", first produced in 1370. This well-known cologne is reputed to have transformed a gout-ridden, paralytic princess in her 70s into a youthful girl desired by the King of Poland — a claim which must have enhanced sales throughout the centuries.

Cultivation

Botanical name: *Rosemarinus officinalis*
Height: 1m (3.3ft). Width 1m (3.3 ft) 8C. A small genus of only three species.A fast-growing, evergreen shrub with silvery green, needle-like leaves. Drought and fire-resistant. Flowers from September to May and occasionally through the summer. Flowers are usually pale lilac but sometimes blue, white, or pink. Endures hot sun and poor soil. Prefers soil with a high lime content.

Propagation

Growing from seed is slow but the plants are easily propagated from stem cuttings or division of the roots. For stem cuttings, break off sprigs 15cm (6in) long with some new growth on them. These can either be placed straight into the ground or potted into a sandy soil and planted out the following spring. Water well until the plant is established. Root division is best done in autumn or early spring.

Pruning

Once established, rosemary grows quickly and soon becomes a woody, straggly plant. Prune in the autumn, but do not cut it back to the old wood. Leave at least a whorl of new growth on the stem. Rosemary makes a good edging plant. Leave 30cm (12in) between each plant and pinch out the growing tips to encourage the plant to spread.

Rosemary and aromatherapy

Rosemary is one of the most important plants used in aromatherapy and is suitable in the treatment of: respiratory problems, colds, headaches, rheumatism and arthritis, stiff joints and muscular pain, heart, liver and gall bladder problems. As a massage oil, add 6 drops of essential oil of rosemary to 1 tablespoon of a carrier oil of your choice.

Infusion: add 1 dessert spoon of leaves or flowers to a cup of boiling water. Leave to stand for 10 minutes. Add honey, if desired. Drink either before or after meals.

Sprigs of rosemary or drops of essential oil can be added to the bath water to help relieve aching joints and muscles. For mental clarity and to assist memory e.g. revising for exams, essential oil can be burned in an incense burner.

N.B.: Rosemary must only be used in small doses. Because it is a stimulant to the brain and nervous system, too much of the herb will over-stimulate and may cause dizziness or epileptic-type fits. Essential oils should never be used by pregnant women, or to treat babies and young children without the advice of a qualified aromatherapy practitioner.

RECIPES

Rosemary vinegar: Place sprigs of rosemary into bottles of wine vinegar and leave to infuse for a few weeks. Makes a good vinegar for salad dressing.

Rosemary butter: Hugh Fearnly-Whittingstall in his River Cottage book suggests the following recipe to accompany fish, in particular red mullet: cream 110g of soft butter with eight mashed anchovy fillets and 1tbsp of finely chopped rosemary.

Lavender: *lavanda*

Lavender is a herb that almost everybody knows something about. Since its introduction to Britain by the Romans, it has been widely used in medicine and toiletries and is the one herb that has never gone out of fashion or lost its popularity. To supply the growing market, fields of lavender were planted in many parts of Britain and some areas, such as Mitcham in Surrey, were famous for their lavender fields. Although still very popular, there was a decrease in demand for lavender throughout the 18th century and many of the lavender fields were dug up. Increasing interest in homeopathy has stimulated a new surge in demand and many of the lavender fields have been re-established.

The name derives from the Latin word *lavare* which means "to wash" and lavender was used throughout the Roman empire to scent bath water and to cleanse wounds. It is native to the Mediterranean but grows easily and prolifically even in cooler northern climates. Its adaptability and ease of cultivation meant that lavender was used throughout the Middle Ages in many areas of daily life and extensively in medicine since the 11th century. It was one of the most popular herbs and was always included in the selection of herbs grown in monastery gardens. The use of lavender water, the first real English perfume, was recommended by many, including the Abbess Hildegard who, writing in the 12th century, advocated it as a good perfume to maintain a "pure character". Lavender has long and strong links with the perfume industry and France is one of the most prolific growers, particularly the region of Provence where the sight and scents of the lavender fields in bloom are truly stunning.

For centuries dried lavender has been placed in small lavender bags used to perfume clothes and linen, with the added advantage that it deters moths. Few people use lavender bags today, although they are growing in popularity, but many people are aware that lavender is an excellent herb to assist sleep and either burn lavender incense in their bedrooms or sleep on lavender pillows. Lavender has a very soothing, balancing effect. It is particularly beneficial to people who suffer from erratic mood swings and has a long history as a tonic for the depressed or hysterical. It stimulates a sense of well-being and helps calm the mind. In common with rosemary and eucalyptus, lavender has antiseptic properties and was strewn around houses to help fight plague and sickness. Along with rosemary, it was used by witches to ward off the evil eye and was one of the herbs dedicated to Hecate, the goddess of witches and sorcerers.

Purple-flowering lavender scents the air in spring. If you take your dog for a walk or hike where goats roam the hills, you will enjoy the strong fragrance released as the animals brush against plants. Even if you are driving through the *campo*, its sudden scent can alert you to the presence of a herd of goats just around the corner — a useful warning signal on those twisting mountain roads. A couple of varieties, rather thin and spindly compared with cultivated lavender, grow wild throughout the Iberian peninsula. One of the commonest is *Lavandula stoechas pendulata*, which is confusingly called "Spanish lavender" and sometimes "French lavender". But this is not to be confused with true French lavender, which is *dentata*, and never to be called "Italian lavender", which is *Lavandula stoechas spp stoechas*. And you thought getting to grips with Spanish grammar was difficult. One of its common names is "rabbit ears" or "butterfly" *(papillon)* and when you look at the flowers it is obvious why as they have wing-shaped bracts growing from the top of the flower stem.

Wild lavender will settle in and spread its seed a long way. It is a useful herb to cultivate on a dry bank or waste ground, providing scent and some colour from spring often through to mid-summer. However, it is not the ideal variety for growing in a border and will not necessarily transplant well. Once cut, the flowers dry easily but they are more brittle than the cultivated varieties and are better used in food or infusions.

Cultivation

Botanical name: *Lavandula stoechas*
A compact, bushy shrub which will grow to 60cm (2ft). Grey-green narrow leaves up to 4cm (1.5 in) long. Purple flowers, occasionally pink, with bracts at the top, grow to 4 cm. Requires full sun and once established survives with very little water.

Propagation

Grows easily from seed or cuttings. Take 7cm (3 in) cuttings in late summer or early autumn and place in pots. They should root and be ready for planting the following spring.

Lavender and aromatherapy

Lavender is an extremely popular oil in aromatherapy. It is very balancing and soothing and also very gentle, one of the few that can be used, in small doses, without diluting it. Particularly good for insomnia, colds, catarrh, headaches, muscular aches and pains, acne and depression.

Few people have an allergic reaction to lavender oil. Those that do are often asthmatic or suffer from hay fever. Those who are allergic often have an "early detection" system: they will dislike the smell and do not wish to be massaged with the oil. Lavender blends well with geranium, citrus, marjoram and rosemary oils. Not only do the smells complement each other but lavender oil acts as a catalyst and increases the efficacy of the oils it is blended with.

CHAPTER 15

FENNEL AND WILD ASPARAGUS

Fennel: *hinojo*

Fennel has been growing wild around the Mediterranean for centuries and there are references to it in Spanish literature as far back as the 1st century AD. Confusion often surrounds this herb, not particularly surprising because there are two very different types. Common fennel *(Foeniculum vulgaris)* is a tall, feathery plant grown for its leaves and seeds, whereas the cultivated fennel (Florence fennel) is chiefly grown for its bulbous base. It is the common fennel you will find around the fields and roadsides of Spain.

Fennel takes its name from the Latin for "little hay". It served as animal fodder, but it has also been used extensively in the culinary and medical fields. Traditionally believed to have protective properties, the herb was hung outside houses to keep witches away. It was also used as an antidote for all forms of poisoning, snake bites, poisonous mushrooms etc. Yet again, scientific research has confirmed what traditional medicine already knew: fennel has powerful anti-toxic properties and inhibits the buildup of toxins in the body. Fennel is good for purging the body of impurities and keeping it "flowing". It aids digestion, constipation, breaks down kidney stones and can be helpful in treating gout. Think of fennel when you think of wanting the body to flow well and you will realise that it is a useful herb for treating menstrual problems and stimulating the flow of milk in nursing mothers.

Its strong anti-toxic properties have led to fennel being used to treat cases of alcohol poisoning and it is sometimes incorporated into rehabilitation programmes. For those on slimming diets, fennel may be a miracle herb because it not only suppresses the appetite but its ability to rid the body of

toxins means it can assist in eliminating cellulite, which is a buildup of toxic waste. As with all homeopathic remedies, it is a case of all things in moderation and too much fennel can have a narcotic, disturbing effect on the body.

This amazing herb, growing up to three metres high, is green with feathery leaves which die down in mid-summer and reappear in autumn. Fennel is an umbeliferous plant, which indicates that its flower heads look like small umbrellas. They are flat on top, about 10cm (4in) wide and contain tiny yellow flowers which give way to the very aromatic seed. The oval-shaped seeds are ready for harvesting when they harden and turn a grey-green colour. At this stage the easiest way to catch the seeds is by cutting off the flower head and hanging it upside down with a paper bag around it so that the seeds drop into the bag as they ripen and fall. If you want to cultivate fennel, it is easily grown from seed. Find a sunny spot and sow the seeds in early spring approximately 30cm (12in) apart. It will soon shoot up and self-sow, but you can divide the main plant every two to three years if you want. Once established, fennel does not need any watering. It is very similar to dill, although the two herbs have quite different tastes. Plant them close together and they are likely to cross-pollinate, producing a less aromatic plant.

Uses of fennel

Fennel is generally known as the "fish herb" and is an excellent accompaniment to all fish dishes. The leaves can be chopped and added to sauces or the seeds cooked with the fish.

ASPARAGUS

Plant: *espárrago*
Food: *espárragos*

Rain brings a change of activity in the *campo*. Work stops and when the rain ceases you will see groups of people wandering around with carrier bags. Look in their bags and you find them full of snails. A few years ago a neighbour invited us to dinner and fed us snails. They felt we would enjoy the meal more knowing that they were "our" snails. A few days after the rains the carrier bags are abandoned and the countryside is littered with people risking life and limb for wild asparagus. I was once delayed by a Guardia Civil car, abandoned on a narrow track with the doors wide open. Unable to pass and assuming the guards had rushed away for some emergency, I waited patiently for 20 minutes. Then two guards returned, looking very sheepish. It was difficult for them to hide the evidence: each carried large bunches of wild asparagus and in pursuit of their quarry had obviously lost track of time.

Wild asparagus has long been a delicacy in Spain and as early as the 16th century recipes were included in such cookery books as Diego Granado's *Libro del Arte de Cocina.* After cultivated asparagus, you may find wild asparagus an acquired taste. The stalks are dark green and slender with a tougher texture than the cultivated variety, but the big difference is the taste. Wild asparagus has a more intense, bitter flavour which may not appeal to all, but I found it a taste worth acquiring and now consider cultivated asparagus rather bland.

Asparagus is probably growing wild all over your land, but where do you find it and how do you recognise it? You have to be quick. Once the rains come, asparagus shoots can appear within 24 hours and when the season starts local people, who have been walking these hillsides for years and know exactly where the best clumps are, respond quickly. They will empty your field of asparagus within an hour, which can be a bit devastating if you have been nurturing a few prime specimens, waiting for just the right moment. When I first came to live in Spain, I was told that anyone had a legal right to cross land if they were collecting snails or picking asparagus. Since then I have made numerous inquiries with the powers that be, but they have been particularly evasive, neither admitting nor denying the truth of this. While you have the right to stop anyone trespassing on your land, people like to keep their options open in terms of traditional freedom of movement — and the collection of free food. As far as I am concerned they can help themselves to as many snails as they like, but I have had more than one argument with strangers homing in on our asparagus.

The plant is spindly and pale-green (very much like an asparagus fern) with extremely spiky stems, which are the older asparagus spears. The shoots to pick are the young tender ones, which look exactly like thinner, greener versions of cultivated asparagus. You must catch them before they become woody, thorny and inedible. You need to be vigilant, as one day they may seem too small to pick and the next they have shot up and gone beyond the edible phase. Cut the stems as close to the ground as possible and scrape off any spikes with a sharp knife. Asparagus spears can be cooked in water, but they have a better flavour and texture if you break them into small pieces and cook them for a few minutes in melted butter. Wild asparagus is wonderful in omelettes, as a sauce for pasta with parmesan and olive oil, or even blended into soup.

RECIPES

Asparagus soup

> 450g (1lb) asparagus
> 50g (2 oz) butter
> 1 small onion, sliced
> 1 stick celery chopped
> 1.15 litres (2 pints) water
> 3 egg yolks
> 240ml (8floz) single cream
> 25g (1oz) cornflour
> salt and pepper
> juice and rind of one lemon (optional)

Remove the tips of each spear and reserve them for garnish. Cut the stalks into small pieces. Heat the butter and saute the onion, celery and asparagus for four minutes. Add water, bring to the boil and simmer 15 minutes. Strain off the liquid and place the vegetables into a blender with a small amount of the liquid. Blend to a purée. Return the liquid to the saucepan and add the purée. Reheat and season to taste. In a bowl blend the cornflour, egg yolks and cream to a smooth mixture. Add a cup of the soup from the saucepan to the bowl, stir well and then blend all this mixture into the soup in the saucepan. Reheat to boiling point and adjust seasoning. Boil the asparagus tips in lightly boiling water for six minutes. If you wish to add lemon juice and rind, do so just before serving. Pour the soup into individual bowls and garnish with the asparagus tips.

CHAPTER 16
GRAPES

Grape: *uva*
Grapevine: *vid or parra*

No Spanish *finca* would be complete without at least one grapevine. The practical combination of a fast-growing shade for summer which sheds its leaves to let light through in autumn and winter, plus the additional benefits of fruit and wine, cannot be ignored. Vines are a gift from the gods and throughout history wine has been lauded as one of the great joys of life. The Old Testament Book of Ecclesiasticus affirms: "What life is then to a man that is without wine? For it was made to make men glad." Wine has long been fundamental to the agriculture, economy and pleasure of many Mediterranean countries.

Spain became one of the first countries to develop a tradition of viticulture when the Phoenicians established commercial vineyards between 900-120BC in the Málaga and Valencia regions. Málaga's rich sweet wine, produced from Muscat grapes, achieved world fame. Known to the Romans as *Malacena vinum*, it continued to be popular during the Moorish occupation of Spain when it was renamed "Málaga syrup", with the implication that it was free of alcohol and therefore could be consumed by teetotallers. Málaga wine acquired a global reputation for excellence and its popularity reached a pinnacle in the19th century. Sadly, devastation caused to the vines by the *phylloxera* bug and changing consumer tastes led to its decline in the 20th century.

The raisin industry, which naturally evolved from the vineyards, was also established by the Phoenicians and raisins remain a fundamental part of the Spanish diet and economy.

Some parts of Spain have a climate ideally suited to drying grapes and raisins quickly became one of the country's chief exports to Greece and Rome, where raisins were so highly prized that two jars of raisins could be traded for one boy slave. Trade outside Mediterranean countries was slower to develop because shipping conditions were poor and raisins are particularly difficult to pack and transport. By the 11th century

conditions had improved and raisins were exported to Northern Europe, a trade stimulated by knights returning from the Crusades. During their travels through the Mediterranean they enjoyed raisins and created a demand for them when they returned to their homelands. Raisins became an increasingly important part of English cuisine but remained phenomenally expensive because all attempts to dry grapes in England failed, obviously due to the cold, wet climate. Missionaries took raisins from Spain to the New World where vineyards were successfully established. The San Joaquin valley near the Sierra Nevada mountains had a perfect climate for growing grapes and the seeds were sown for the lucrative Californian wine and raisin industry. In 1876, at the Maryville District Fair, the public was introduced to the first seedless grapes, developed by a Scottish immigrant, William Thompson. The thin-skinned, sweet Lady deCoverley grape fulfilled an enormous demand (from chefs and those with false teeth) for seedless raisins.

In 1863 catastrophe struck European vineyards, almost ending wine production, when acres of vines were infested with *Phylloxera vastratrix*. *Phylloxera* is a louse that attacks the roots of vines causing leaves to drop and the plant's eventual death. The bug arrived in France from America and spread very quickly throughout Europe. American vineyards were not affected by the bug and it was discovered that their vines were resistant to *phylloxera*. Salvation came to Europe when grafting European grapes on to the rootstock of American vines produced a hybrid that was resistant to *phylloxera*. Lately, it has been discovered that at least two different types of *phylloxera* and one rootstock originally believed to be resistant succumb to the bug after producing grapes for about 20 years. The wheel has now turned full circle, with the louse that travelled to Europe from America returning to its homeland and creating problems for American wine producers. Many extremely productive vineyards were established during the 1960s and heavily planted with what is now known to be vulnerable rootstock. As a result, a large number of wine producers face the costly task of replanting acres of vines.

The *Ruta de la Pasa* (Route of the Raisins) in Andalusia takes the traveller inland to the picturesque, white, hill-top village of Comares and a landscape dotted with *paseros*, raisin beds. Usually placed on south-west facing slopes to take advantage of as much sun as possible, the beds have white, pointed headstones, rather like those in graveyards. Towards the end of August and in the first couple of weeks of September, ripe grapes are spread over the beds. The bunches are turned regularly to ensure they dry evenly, while the farmers pray for a few weeks of hot sun before the autumn rains. In the event of rain or to protect the raisins against heavy dew, tent-like tarpaulins are pulled over these *paseros* without touching the fruit. Once covered, the drying crop should survive a day or two of rain, but continuous moisture and high levels of humidity will turn the grapes mouldy and herald the end of the raisin crop for that year. All is not lost because, if they are caught in time, the crop can be turned into superb wine but there is a significant drop in income for the producers.

You may have inherited a vine with your house. If not, it is worth planting at least one, which can provide you with all you need in terms of table grapes. And why not try drying them so you have raisins for the winter months? If you plan to make your own wine, you may need a few more vines, depending how much you like to drink. As a rough guide, a healthy, established vine will produce about 25 kilos (55lbs) of fruit and 5-7 kilos (11-15lbs) will make 4.5 litres (one gallon) of wine. If you are planting vines, you need to consider the different grape varieties. It is easy to grow vines from cuttings but, if you want to plant different types to those that you or your neighbours already have, such as seedless grapes, most garden centres are well stocked. Quite likely, vines already established on your land will be suitable for making *vino del terreno*, as local wine is known. Producing wine from grapes grown in hot climates is considerably easier than the complicated process employing the wine-making kits available in the UK because the high quantity of sugar contained in the skin of the fruit speeds and enhances the fermentation process.

The first year we attempted to make our own *vino del terreno*, my son in law insisted on treading the grapes himself because he was not going to drink wine produced by anyone else's pounding feet. We all paled at the thought and insisted that we weren't prepared to drink anything his feet had been in contact with. He prevailed, however, and when the wine was ready he pronounced it so exquisite that curiosity got the better of us. "Exquisite" was a slight exaggeration, but the wine was certainly quaffable. Many of our neighbours have wellington boots that are used solely for crushing grapes, but purists say that the best wines come from grapes crushed with bare feet. On a recent trip to Portugal we visited Taylor's port lodge in Oporto where most grapes are now crushed mechanically, but Taylor's state that their best port is indeed made from grapes trodden by (clean!) feet. A few men start treading the grapes and the process develops into a fiesta, ending with couples dancing around in the grape juice. Many areas of Spain have fiestas to celebrate the *vendimia*, grape harvest, and they are not to be missed. As well as seeing how the local wine is made, there are plentiful opportunities for sampling it.

CULTIVATION
Propagating and transplanting vines

Select a variety suitable for either eating or wine-making. A number of grape types flourish in southern Spain. In Málaga the moscatel, or muscat, is grown both for the table and, along with Pedro Ximénez grapes, for making wine. Pedro Ximénez also dominates the Montilla-Moriles vineyards in Córdoba province, which produce sherry-type wines of high alcoholic content. Sherry, made in Cádiz province, comes largely from the palomino grape. Huelva makes light white wines using the zalema grape. Across the region, several bodegas are experimenting with other vine varieties to produce very drinkable reds. Plant any time from November until February. If you are transplanting vines with established root systems, dig a hole that is twice the width of the root-ball and at least as deep. Although vines are tolerant of almost any type of soil, they dislike standing in water so ensure the soil drains well. To help drainage line the bottom of the planting hole with stones, gravel or broken pots. Loosen the roots by teasing them out of the root-ball and, if the soil is very dry, soak the vine in water for at least an hour before planting. If planting a large number of vines in rows, allow about two metres between each plant and a couple of metres between each row. Once the vines are planted, water them well.

Growing vines from cuttings

Vines can be grown very easily from cuttings. If you have an established vine you should prune it in spring and it is simplicity itself to plant some of the prunings. Cuttings can be either dormant hardwood or young, green cuttings, which are quick to establish. Dormant cuttings, the easiest to grow, can be taken any time between the leaves dropping and the buds starting to grow. Choose a shoot that has grown during the recent growing season. Any healthy section of vine with a diameter of 2cm (3/4in) should do well, but the best vines will be produced from cuttings taken from where the cane branches away from the main stem and which are still green inside and have at least three buds, or nodes. The strongest roots will grow from the nodes so the more nodes in a cutting the better the chances of producing a good root system. Discard any cuttings that are spongy or have yellowing or dark wood. Cuttings should be 30-45cm (12-18in) long and the top cut should be at least 1.5cm (1/2in) above the bud. Once you have chopped off lots of stems from the vine it may become difficult to identify one end of a cutting from the other. The best technique is to make different types of cuts at the tops and bottoms of the cuttings, for example, straight across at the bottom and a diagonal cut at the top or vice versa. Whatever you choose, remain consistent or you won't know which end to stick in the ground when the time comes.

Green (softwood) cuttings

Some varieties of grape do not root well from dormant cuttings and younger, green cuttings are needed. Take the cuttings in spring from any young vigorous shoot. They should be 10-15cm (4-6 in) long with two or three leaves. Remove all but the top leaf. The cuttings need at least one leaf to help them grow. Dip the cutting in rooting hormone and plant in rich, well-drained soil. Keep in a warm place until the cutting produces roots after which it can be transplanted into the ground.

After- -care

Grapes are very tolerant of soil and weather conditions and need very little attention once they are established. However, a little extra attention will give you the best fruit possible and, whether you intend to eat them or make wine, you want plump, juicy grapes. There are three main times to provide water: while the roots are becoming established, when the flowers are forming and later in the season when the fruit is swelling.

Fertilising

Vines do not require much in the way of fertiliser. If you really feel that they need encouragement, add a small amount of manure to the soil in spring. But usually they will grow quite well without.

Pruning

To produce well, grapevines must be pruned every year, in February or March. How you prune them will depend on whether you want wine or shade and table grapes. For wine-making, prune vines into a low-growing bush. For standard vines, in the first year select the strongest branches and prune them back to four buds. In the second year prune to eight buds. As spring moves into summer continue to maintain the vine by cutting off any weak branches and pinching out any side shoots that are not needed.

Pests and diseases

Vines grown outdoors tend to be more resistant to pests and diseases than those grown in greenhouses. But they are at the mercy of the weather, which creates its own problems. Rain at the wrong time can result in mildew problems. The year 2004 was disastrous due to too much rain late in the season. Many farmers lost the whole of their crop and Spain's ability to fulfil its quota in order to qualify for European subsidies was in doubt. Failure to do so results in a loss of subsidies for subsequent years.

Once the growing season has started, vines prefer hot, dry conditions and do not respond well to moisture or humidity. To prevent mould, grapes are treated with a sprinkling of sulphur (*azufre*), purchased from local hardware stores or agricultural suppliers, and should be applied from February onwards. Not surprisingly, throwing sulphur around can be highly dangerous and should never be undertaken on windy days, in very hot sun or if children are playing nearby. Sprinkling techniques vary. One highly recommended method is to put the sulphur in an old sock (or a new one if you are very particular) and shake it over the vine. A neighbour of mine insisted on lending me his "machine" for applying sulphur. I was intrigued, expecting a state-of-the-art piece of equipment, and was highly impressed when he turned up with an old tomato tin, holes pierced in the bottom and a piece of string around the top. The sulphur was placed in the can and then shaken over the vine, simple and effective.

Wasps and birds can be pests, particularly when the grapes are ripening. You may be able to cover the whole vine with netting. If not, cover individual bunches of grapes with bags until they are ready to be picked. Refer to Chapter 18 (pests and diseases) for further information on botrytis, grey mould, mildew and vine weevils.

RECIPES

Grape juice

If you don't drink alcohol or don't want the hassle of making wine, making grape juice is extremely easy. Use bunches of black grapes picked from the stem. Put them in a large saucepan and cover with cold water. Boil them until the skins begin to split. Strain the juice twice, through a filter or fine muslin. To every 2 cups of juice add 1/2 cup sugar. Boil the juice and sugar for 20 minutes. When cool, bottle the juice. Keep refrigerated, or you can freeze it.

CHAPTER 17

WALNUTS AND CHESTNUTS

Walnut (tree and wood): *nogal*
Nut: *nuez*

As you travel through cooler, wetter parts of Spain or climb the higher slopes of the mountain ranges, olive and almond trees slowly give way to a different botanical landscape. Pine forests become more prolific and then you can spot the wonderful, luxuriant growth of walnut and chestnut trees. Native to south eastern Europe and Asia, walnut trees were planted throughout Europe by the Romans. A traditional emblem of love and marriage, walnuts were believed to bring fertility, which resulted in the potentially painful Roman custom of throwing the nuts at couples after the wedding ceremony — you can understand why confetti became a more popular option. For the bride, however, receiving a blow from a walnut may have been just the beginning of her marital problems when you consider the old English proverb "A woman, a dog and a walnut tree/The more you beat them the better they be."

As well as their association with fertility, walnuts were endowed with mystical properties, not all of which were good. It was believed that the black walnut tree (*Juglans nigra*) attracted lightning and because of this the wood was spurned by shipbuilders. You may wonder why only ship-builders refused to use it. Would you want it in your house? Whatever the truth of the matter, there is an unusually high recorded incidence of cattle being struck by lightning when sheltering under black walnut trees. On the positive side, walnut reputedly repels insects and walnut leaves were scattered around stables and outside houses. During the Middle Ages coachmen rubbed their horses down with a solution of water in which walnut leaves had been steeped. Culpepper recommends an infusion of the leaves to kill worms in the stomach and apparently this infusion is also effective if you are bitten by rabid dogs. He advises that the nuts are most potent when unripe and green and that the nuts become oily and unpalatable with age, but recommends that an older kernel, when taken with red wine, "stays the falling of the hair and makes it fair". In fact, pressed walnuts produce a yellow dye, frequently used in the manufacture of soap and paint, as well as a rich, unsaturated oil excellent for cooking.

Research continues producing new evidence that a diet rich in nuts is excellent for reducing the risk of heart disease. In 2004, research results were published showing that the oil contained in walnuts converts to Omega 3 fatty acids, similar to fish oils, which help reduce inflammation and arteriosclerosis.

Although all species of walnut trees produce edible nuts, some have thicker shells than others and are more difficult to crack. Many, such as the black walnut, are primarily grown for their wood and the fruit's hard, thick shells are often used in the manufacture of plastics, as anti-skid agents in tyres and in metal polishers. The species most widely grown throughout Europe for its fruit is *Juglans regia*, sometimes called the Persian or English walnut, which produces large nuts that are relatively easy to crack. Walnuts are not just about the ripe hard nuts we associate with Christmas; in many countries young, green walnuts are considered a delicacy. Green walnuts can be pickled and are delicious added to salads, as an ingredient in casseroles or as an accompaniment to pheasant.

A very slow-growing tree, walnut produces a beautiful, hard wood very much in demand by cabinet-makers. One species the tree, if damaged, grows a burr along the branches and down the trunk which creates a wonderful, streaked pattern in the wood, highly sought by carpenters for veneer. One long-standing association that may spring to mind when you think of walnut veneer is that with luxury cars. Walnut is used in many cars such as Bentleys.

However, walnut may not be the tree to plant if you want wood in a hurry. John Seymour in his book on self-sufficiency describes walnut as the king of woods but warns that it is not ready to harvest for at least 150 years and that it's best to wait 350 years "if you have the patience for it". I suspect that patience may not be the biggest problem.

Cultivation

Botanical name: *Juglans deciduous*
Hardy. The common walnut, *Juglans regia*, is one of the faster growing species reaching heights of about 30 metres (100ft). Walnuts have separate male and female flowers on the same tree and are wind-pollinated. Male flowers appear in early summer as yellowish-green catkins. Female flowers grow in clusters and are almost leafless, followed by round, green fruit growing to 5cm (2in) in diameter, which contain the edible nut. Trees start to produce fruit from about eight years old. Walnuts tolerate quite low temperatures but do not like extremely high temperatures.

Aftercare

Although established trees will survive without summer water, the trees need sufficient deep watering to produce a good crop of fruit. Walnut trees have very deep roots so make sure that you give them enough water to penetrate well below the surface and reach the roots.

Harvesting

If you want green fruit for pickling, pick them before they ripen but are soft enough for a needle to pierce them easily. To get the best edible nuts, leave the fruit on the tree as long as possible to ripen. Unlike many other nuts, walnuts do not split open, but the outer casing rots away to reveal the nut inside. Dried nuts keep well for several months when stored in dry conditions at room temperature.

RECIPES

Pickled walnuts

Wash young, green walnuts and prick them all over with a needle or fork. Make enough brine solution to cover them. Brine solution: Add 150gm of salt to each litre of water. Boil it and leave to cool. Keep the walnuts in brine solution for one week, draining them and making a fresh batch of the solution every two days. Rinse in fresh water and spread them to dry for a couple of days, then pack them in jars with hot pickling vinegar. Seal jars and leave in a dark place for at least one month, but preferably three months, before eating. Will keep for two to three years.

Walnut liqueur

An unusual black liqueur very popular in France, where it is called *brou*. The following amounts are only a guide and the recipe can be adapted to suit your personal taste. Pick green walnuts at the same stage as you would for pickling (see section on harvesting). To each 1/2 litre of brandy add 6 quartered walnuts. Place the nuts and brandy in a bottling jar, cover tightly and leave for two months. Add 6oz sugar, 1/2in piece of cinnamon stick and leave for another month. Strain off the liqueur and bottle it. You can make walnut wine, *vin de noix,* by simply adding a large wineglass of the liqueur (or to taste) to a litre of red wine.

SWEET CHESTNUT

Tree, wood: *castaño*
Fruit: *castaña*

The sweet chestnut tree is also known as "Spanish chestnut", although the tree originally takes its name from Catanis in

Thessaly where it grew abundantly. It is a true giant among trees and can reach 30 metres (100ft) in height with a spread of 15 metres (50ft). Chestnut trees are magnificent and extremely ornamental, particularly when they are dripping with glorious-coloured catkins. It is the female parts of the flowering catkins that give way to the spine-covered chestnuts. The British associate chestnuts with Christmas, turkey with chestnut stuffing being one of the classic Christmas recipes, and the smell of chestnuts roasting on winter evenings is very evocative. But in many Mediterranean countries, particularly France and Italy, chestnuts have long been a staple part of the diet, so much so that in the 12th century chestnut trees were called "bread trees". The delicious fruit are also nutritious, being high in many vitamins, particularly vitamin C.

The nuts were fundamental to numerous aspects of country folk's lives. Unlike most other nuts, chestnuts do not contain much oil, but they do have higher quantities of complex carbohydrates which create the dense consistency appropriate for such products as flour. Italy still has many mills where chestnuts are ground into flour, *farina de castagne*, in increasing demand because it is gluten-free. In Italy and Corsica, chestnut flour is used to make bread, pastries, polenta and, in some areas, beer is brewed from chestnuts.

Although traditionally a peasant food, the humble chestnut is elevated to something grander by the French. They favour larger chestnuts, known as *marrons,* which have a higher sugar content than other varieties and make excellent chestnut *purée*.

Both the fruit and the puree are used in many well-known traditional French desserts but the chestnut moves into the luxury category in the form of the Christmas sweetmeat *marron glacé.* Creating this dessert is a long, labour-intensive process. The best chestnuts are selected, peeled and steamed, immersed in syrup for a couple of days and glazed with icing sugar. Not too time-consuming you may think, but this process is repeated again, and again, and again — sometimes as many as a dozen times — before the fruit becomes that perfectly glazed, translucent *marron glacé* which melts in the mouth.

So, an excellent dietary staple and an expensive sweetmeat. But, if you have read the preceding chapters, you will know that most trees offer a wide range of useful qualities and the chestnut is no exception. It has long been one of Europe's best sources of tannin and is still the main source in Italy, particularly for treating leather destined for the manufacture of shoes. In the clothing industry, chestnut meal was used as a bleach for linen and also as a starch. The good, durable timber is used in building, even though it tends to split as it ages, and has been used extensively in carpentry and panelling. Young chestnut trees contain less sap than most growing trees, which means that the wood is harder and not flexible. The trees are fast-growing and the small trunks are excellent for poles, particularly for stakes and fences. Chestnut was the traditional wood used for pit-props and hop poles. To supply the demand for these, chestnut trees are often coppiced to create many small trunks rather than one large one. The wood is also used to make yokes, wine-barrels, railway sleepers, the list is endless.

Chestnut leaves also have applications in the field of medicine. An infusion of leaves was often recommended to treat respiratory problems, fevers and coughs, particularly convulsive coughs such as whooping cough. In Spain chestnut was believed to help ward off the evil eye and leaves were placed under mattresses to protect the sleeper during the night. Chestnuts were also used as a charm against rheumatism but only, apparently, if the nuts were either stolen or begged. Although called "Spanish chestnut", this country originally being one of Europe's largest producers of chestnuts, the last 20 years has seen a decline in demand, particularly in the domestic market, with France and Italy forging ahead. Falling revenues have resulted in neglected trees and the depletion of the forests. Towards the end of the last century some companies, such as Sierra Rica in Aracena (Huelva province), took action to save the chestnut forests and started to reverse declining sales by producing organic products, such as chestnut purée. Demand is growing and the next decade will hopefully see the return of a thriving chestnut industry in Spain.

Cultivation

Botanical name: *Castanea sativa*
A large, wide tree up to 30 metres (100ft) high, 15 metres (50ft) wide. Large, glossy, narrow leaves, slightly leathery in texture. The leaves grow to about 23cm (9in) long and taper to points. Flowers arranged in catkins have both male and female flowers and are wind-pollinated.

Planting

Plant in well-drained soil. Avoid very exposed situations and windy sites. Although the tree is deep-rooted and, once established, will survive the wind, its large leaves cause it to suffer quickly from water loss. Chestnut trees will grow in hot climates, but high summer temperatures cause the fruit to deteriorate quickly and they are unlikely to produce plump chestnuts.

Irrigation

Chestnuts are drought resistant but prefer some summer water. They do not like to stand in water and doing so may result in rot so make sure that the soil is light and well drained. Drip irrigation is the most appropriate form of irrigation for chestnut trees.

Fertilising

If the tree does not seem to be thriving, fertilise in the second year of growth with a nitrogen-phosphorous-potash fertiliser and then every three years.

Propagation

Budding or grafting is the best way. Chestnuts can be grown from seed. The seeds must be kept at between 0-2C for two months to break dormancy and planted at a depth of 7cm (2.5in).

Harvesting

Collect the fruit from the ground every couple of days and remove them from the spiky burrs as soon as possible.

Pruning

Chestnuts do not need any specialised pruning. Unless you want to coppice them to make fencing poles, concentrate on encouraging a strong leader and remove any low growing branches from the main trunk. When the tree is young, prune any crossing branches and remove any limbs that are damaged. Otherwise, the tree should look after itself.

Uses

For coughs and fevers, infuse 1oz of dried leaves in one pint of boiling water and allow to cool. Drink anything from one tablespoonful to a wineglass full three times a day.

Cooking with chestnuts

Before using chestnuts in a recipe you have to peel them, which may seem a daunting task but is quite simple. Bring a large pan of water to the boil. Make a slit down the side of each chestnut, place them in the boiling water and boil them for about 10 minutes. Drain the water and allow the chestnuts to cool. You should then be able to peel away both skins quite easily.

RECIPES

Chestnut purée
   675g chestnuts
   720ml milk
   dash of vanilla extract
   100g softened butter
   225g granulated sugar
   240 ml water

Place peeled chestnuts in a saucepan with milk and vanilla and cook over a moderate heat for 45 minutes or until tender. Drain, reserving a little of the liquid. Place in a food processor, add a little of the liquid and process until smooth. Add the butter and mix thoroughly. Place sugar and water in a saucepan and bring to boil over a moderate heat, stirring constantly until sugar dissolves. Boil for 8 minutes to form a syrup, but do not let it brown. Stir the hot syrup into the chestnut mixture.

Chestnut soup
    1 medium carrot, sliced
    1 medium onion, sliced
    1 finely chopped rasher of bacon (optional)
    500g peeled chestnuts
    25g butter
    1/2 litre chicken stock
    1/4 litre single cream
    1 sprig each of parsley and thyme
    1 bay leaf
    salt and pepper
    garnish colon: 1 desert apple, peeled, cored and sliced,
    0.25g butter,
    1 tablespoon brown sugar

Fry bacon in butter, add chestnuts and vegetables. Stir and cook gently until onions soften. Add stock and herbs. Simmer gently for 25-35 minutes until chestnuts are tender. Blend in a processor. Add cream. Garnish melt remaining butter in a pan. Add sugar and dissolve slowly. Add sliced apple and allow to caramelise slightly. Place on top of soup.

CHAPTER 18

FIRE AND WATER

Andalusia's countryside is one of extremes. The searing heat of summer can quickly give way to monsoon-like rain and several years of drought may be followed by a couple of winters of damaging floods. It always seems as though we are in some type of crisis situation. In Andalusia and other areas of Spain, a water management programme during the last decade has helped to reduce storm damage, with the installation of dams, culverts, and correct drainage on roads. Hopefully these measures will bring to an end the terrible memories we have of friends, houses and cars being washed away in floods.

Moving from the wider picture to the more personal, it can be frustrating dealing with water. Sometimes it feels as though we have spent all winter battening down the hatches: several weeks of torrential rain resulting in overflowing rivers, impassable tracks, damp wood that refuses to yield a degree of heat, wet clothes everywhere and water rising up through the kitchen floor. Such a winter can be followed by a summer of drought: dry wells, no mains water for three months and daily trips to the local spring, while the plants so carefully nurtured and saved from drowning in the winter finally give up the fight and die of dehydration. This is no exaggeration, but I wouldn't want to live anywhere else, which is probably grounds for a visit from the men in white coats.

In 16 years I have experienced three such winters, including a seven-year period of increasing summer drought. During one such summer I explored all methods of water conservation and discovered the theories of "permaculture" (PERMAnent

agriCULTURE), evolved by Tasmanian Bill Mollison. This
focuses on intensive, labour-efficient, small-scale systems of
food production and animal husbandry on the basis that the
working relationships of plants, animals and people are
fundamentally interconnected. Bill´s theory works on the
lines of "how to grow all your food on less than two litres
of water a day"- nice idea, but we didn´t even have two
litres. However, given that subsequent summers have not
been quite as bad as that of 1995, it has been worth putting
many of his ideas into practice because so much water
which could beutilised to irrigate the garden goes to waste.

Most trees will survive through the summer without
water, the exceptions being fruit trees. You can re-use water
from your house for both household and irrigation purposes,
e.g. using water from the washing machine to service the
toilet. To do this thoroughly, you need to install plumbing
systems for re-using and storing water. As it takes some
planning, I suggest you either read up on it first or contact
the agencies listed in the appendices. But it's quite easy to
harness water in other ways. Installing guttering to channel
rainwater is probably the simplest, but it's also easy to store
water from the bath or the washing machine for re-use on
your land.

Drilling a well is an alternative. You need permission from
your local town hall and the hidrology department. Some of
the drilling companies will obtain the necessary permissions
for you. They will send a representative to examine your
land and decide where to drill. Sometimes this is fairly
obvious. Vegetation can often indicate underground water,
e.g. eucalyptus trees or reeds. They may also send a water
diviner to scour the area. Once drilling begins, the noisy
operation will cover everything in sight with disgusting
layers of dust, turning your land into a moonscape. Water
may be found very quickly, in which case you have no
problems. But, if water isn't found, you will have to make a
decision about whether to drill deeper. Drilling companies'
charges vary according to whether water is found or not.

If you do hit water, you may have to line the well,

depending on the type of earth and rock. Then the well is capped. Once you have installed the pump, with luck you can sit back and enjoy an unlimited supply of sweet water. It can be satisfying to have your own well, but there are no guarantees that water will be found or that there will be a plentiful supply. Thus, it can be a costly, unproductive process. Good luck, and if all else fails there's always the water from the rain, the washing machine, the shower…

Fire

The number of forest and *campo* fires seems to have increased alarmingly over recent years and heavier fines and prison sentences have been imposed on the culprits, regardless of whether the fire was started accidentally or deliberately. Although some fires are started deliberately by insane people, many I have witnessed result from thoughtlessness and lack of awareness of the danger. Not only people burning rubbish on windy days put our lives at risk. Fires can be started in unimaginable ways. I witnessed an Englishman using a petrol strimmer in summer, presumably with the admirable intention of getting rid of potentially dangerous dry scrub. Unfortunately, he didn't realise that strimmers can create sparks when the wire hits rock. Soon he set fire to the scrub, panicked and dropped the petrol strimmer on the burning plants, literally fuelling the flames. I have heard of fires started by cars with catalytic converters driving through them, again sparks igniting the scrub.

Whether burning prunings or scrub, you need to be responsible. Out-of-control fires are a continual threat, particularly from May to October when the whole countryside is like a tinder box. For whatever reason you wish to light a fire outdoors, you must apply for permission. In my region permission is regulated by the Junta de Andalucia via the local town hall. Because the local authority has to allocate resources if fires get out of control, they need to be aware of who is lighting what and where. Not only may they need fire engines, helicopters or ambulances, they also must have resources available to combat blazes started by the odd idiot throwing a cigarette end out of a car window.

Your local town hall makes no charge for giving permission to burn rubbish or scrub, but you do have to complete a form. You are required to identify your property, easily done with your *plan catastral* or the *número catastral,* and provide some personal information. A sample form is available at the end of the chapter. Once completed, the form is faxed to the Junta and permission is usually available within a few hours of your application being submitted.

Make sure you ask for a contact phone number in case of emergencies and, if you have a mobile phone, put the number in the memory and keep it to hand while you are at the fire. This may sound fairly obvious advice, but we have been phoned by people in a panic because they have an out-of-control fire and don't know whom to contact, or what to say to them. The 20 minutes it may take you to get back to the house and locate a phone number can be disastrous.

Areas of the province are divided into high, medium and low-risk areas, some of which may not be granted permission at all in summer months. The rules regarding permission for fires change within different areas but effectively include the following points:

Permission is required all year, not only during summer.

Unless there are very special circumstances, permission will only be given for fires on weekdays, not weekends or fiestas.

Fires can only be lit during specified hours.

You must have a source of water close to the fire.

A responsible person must be in attendance at all times and, if you cannot be there until the fire is completely dead, you must specify on the form who will be in charge and provide their details.

If burning scrub, you must inform your neighbours in advance.

Once you have permission, you have a fixed period in which

to carry out the burning. It may be 24 hours or three days, depending on what you are burning and the permission granted. This is because you cannot guarantee that the weather will be appropriate on the day designated. It may be raining, but the worst enemy is strong wind and even if you have permission never — ever — underestimate the danger. Failure to comply with the regulations for lighting fires can result in a heavy fine and imprisonment.

contaminad...
icada.
gua al menos durante 15 minutos.
gua y jabón, sin frotar.

oso
poral.
era necesario, respiración artificial.
ante, acuéstela de lado con la cabeza
uerpo y las rodillas semiflexionadas.
centro hospitalario, y siempre que sea
el envase.

ICADO EN NINGUN CASO.

EXTREMADAMENTE
INFLAMABLE

CHAPTER 19
PESTS AND DISEASES

It is impossible to live in the countryside without encountering pests and diseases — and the numerous chemicals used to combat them. When I first came to Spain, farmers still used traditional farming methods in line with the principles of organic systems of land management. Later came a dramatic rise in the use of chemical pesticides. It was difficult to ignore all those strips of plastic tied to trees warning us of toxins or the numerous planes flying over in spring, spraying noxious chemicals across the land. It wasn't just the widespread use of chemicals that was worrying but it appeared that Spain permitted chemicals already banned in other European countries, and many farmers used them prolifically thinking "more is better".

The past decade has brought tighter controls and even a move back to traditional farming methods and organic principles by many farmers and their advisory bodies. Spanish ecological associations have worked hard to raise awareness and achieved a degree of success. In 2004 Andalusia banned crop-spraying by plane and, as an alternative, farmers have been offered advice and free pheromone traps to combat olive fly. The results of this experiment were due to be assessed in 2005.

The Olive Oil Council, which publishes comprehensive manuals on both pests and diseases affecting olives, sums up by suggesting there are so many pests and diseases that farmers should not bother to fight them. This advice is totally in keeping with the principles of organic farming. The implication is that healthy trees are less likely to succumb to attack and, if they do, they will be strong enough to fight. This is good in theory, but new owners may find not-so-healthy trees on their land after they have been neglected for several years, possibly because previous owners were elderly or lived in the city. Some trees succumb but others are hardier. I have found that olive, carob and oak trees are fairly sturdy and keep going through years of neglect whereas almond and citrus are more fragile and require regular attention.

It is beyond the scope of this book to recommend chemical treatments for whatever may be ailing your tree or plant. Permitted chemicals and the rules governing their use change from year to year and, if you wish to go down that route, it is best to consult an expert who will have the most up-to-date information. Agricultural suppliers in small towns stock both chemical and biological products. However, I have heard many people say they cannot identify the problem with their trees, let alone ask for a product to treat it with, so I hope the following list of problems most likely to be encountered will prove useful, along with some organic solutions.

Ants: *hormigas*

Ants are particularly attracted to honeydew, a sticky substance secreted by pests such as mealy-bugs and aphids. Although ants eat multitudes of aphids, they are a mixed blessing and create other problems by carrying pests and diseases between trees. Treatment: You will often see citrus orchards with the tree trunks painted white. This is *cal* (lime) which is applied to discourage insects from crawling up the trunk. If you have ants crawling up and down your tree, the chances are that you have other problems, so inspect the tree thoroughly for aphids, mould, honeydew etc. and treat the underlying problem.

Aphids: *pulgones*

Aphids include the well-known green-fly and black-fly, but come in a variety of other colours, including blue, yellow and pink. One of the most common and troublesome of pests, they attack in large numbers and are easily visible, particularly on young shoots. Aphids quickly suck all the sap from plants, causing leaves to shrivel and curl. They also excrete a sticky substance which may develop a sooty mould. Aphids not only weaken trees and plants but spread viral diseases from one plant to another. They are mostly female and successfully reproduce without the need of a male. Each aphid produces up to 100 young in her short life and each can start reproducing when it is only six days old. It seems a shame to attack this excellent example of female self-sufficiency but, if you want your plants to thrive, attack it you must. Treatment: encourage ladybirds as they consume large numbers of aphids. Each adult ladybird can munch their way through 5,000 aphids in their lifetime. Otherwise, aphids can be wiped off by hand, or hosed off with a powerful spray of water, but if you have a bad infestation treat with insecticidal soap, soft soap, garlic spray, derris or neem.

Bacterial canker: *canker bacteriano*

Generally affects the leaves and bark of *Prunus* species, e.g. almond. In the early stages brown spots develop on leaves in spring and sometimes develop a yellow ring around them. The spots then fall out of the leaf leaving a small hole as though somebody has been over your tree with a tiny hole-puncher. When branches are affected, they exude a sticky gum and the leaves on those stems will turn yellow, shrivel and die. Bacterial canker attacks trees where there is any wounding or scarring. Treatment: Infection occurs in autumn so pruning away any diseased tissue in late summer will help to prevent it. Prune out any branches that cross with other branches and are likely to rub against each other causing wounds. If the disease is already established, cut out affected wood and spray the tree with Bordeaux or Burgundy mixture

Botrytis: *botritiosis*

Also called grey mould, botrytis is caused by the fungus *Botrytis cinerea* which causes grapes to rot. Infected grapes turn soft and watery and become covered in a grey mould. The infection quickly spreads to any grapes touching infected fruit and is particularly active if there is any fruit damaged by birds, insects or mildew and in wet humid conditions. Treatment: prune to ensure good air circulation around the crop. Treat with sulphur, and limit damage to the grapes by birds and wasps with the use of nets.

Citrus leaf miner: *minador de cítricos*

A small grub that mostly lives in the leaves but also attacks new shoots. It "mines" its way through them and can be identified by small silvery tracks running along the leaves. Treatment: apply neem oil every two to three weeks.

Gall wasps: *avispa de agalla*

This is the common name for a group of stinging wasps that attack specific tissues of various plants. Common on oak trees, the wasps also attack all varieties of citrus trees although they are more prevalent in temperate regions. The female wasp lays her eggs between the bark and the wood of the stem causing a swelling as the wasps grow, forming large distortions or galls on the tree. Treatment: once the galls are large and established the only treatment is to remove the tree limb or try to prune out the infected wood and destroy the eggs. As with all pests and diseases, the earlier you catch it the better. If you identify it when the gall is new, you can cut a V-shape into the wood and expose the eggs to the air, which prevents them growing into adults.

Grey mould - see botrytis

Gummosis: *gumosis*

The first symptom of gummosis you will see is small drops of a sticky substance on the bark of the tree. The bark may split slightly and the amount of sticky substance will increase. The cause is not known but gummosis is believed to be associated with damage to the tree. Treatment: there is no known treatment. Diseased branches must be removed but, once it has entered the trunk, there is little that can be done.

Mealybugs: *pulgones*

Small oval-shaped bugs, usually found surrounded by a white woolly coat, they look rather like cotton-wool balls. Frequently found on citrus trees, either on the underside of leaves where they join the stem or attached to the stem itself. Treatment: when small, mealybugs can be wiped from the plant. Larger bugs are easily picked from the tree, but are disgusting to kill because they are gooey and exude a red, sticky substance. Treat each bug with a cotton-wool bud dipped in methylated spirits, *alcohol desnaturalizado,* or insecticidal soap.

Mildew: *mildiu*

Mildew affects many plants, including grapevines. There are two types, downy mildew and powdery mildew (*moho polvoriento*). Whereas powdery mildew stays on the surface, usually the upper leaf, downy mildew penetrates through and can kill the plant. In dry conditions the powdery variety may affect all parts of grapevines, particularly vines grown against walls. The grapes will start to split and may succumb to secondary infections such as botrytis. It helps prevent mildew if you mulch around the plant to retain water. Damp conditions bring their own problems in the form of downy mildew. This will cause leaves and fruit to drop and eventually result in the death of the plant. Again it may also give rise to botrytis. Treatment: dust vines with sulphur. Remove any diseased tissue. In wet conditions improve air circulation around vines by thinning out the fruit and leaves. Use Bordeaux mixture or Burgundy mixture.

Mistletoe: *muérdago*

Mistletoe is a parasitic plant which sucks the water from its host tree. Most likely to attack olive and almond trees, if ignored it will eventually kill the tree. For more information refer to the section on pruning olives in Chapter 10. Treatment: prune out the affected limbs and burn.

Olive fly: *mosca de las aceitunas*

Olive fly *(Dacus oleae)* is a persistent and invasive pest which winters in the soil around olive trees. The adult is 4-5 mm long and produces several hundred offspring in its lifetime. Olive flies insert their eggs under the skin of the fruit causing extensive damage, including premature fruit drop, increase in acidity, and destruction of the olive pulp causing the fruit to shrivel. Treatment: keep the tree healthy and well-pruned to ensure air circulation around the branches. Use pheromone traps.

Peach leaf curl: *enrollamiento de la hoja del melocotón*

A slightly confusing name because it affects all the *prunus* family, not just peach trees, therefore you may see it on your almond trees. A quick glance at the tree reveals a red tinge to the leaves which look as though they are turning autumnal. On closer investigation you will see red blisters on the leaves, which eventually turn white. Peach leaf curl is a fungal disease which undermines trees and causes early leaf drop. Treatment: you can remove individual leaves, but if you have many trees this can be difficult, laborious and possibly not very effective. The spores of peach leaf curl are carried by the rain and the problem is likely to reoccur the following year. Spray with copper fungicide in autumn and again in spring. Repeat four times at intervals of two weeks and spray again at the end of the summer before the leaves begin to fall.

Scale insects: *insectos de la escala*

These small insects are most likely to be found along the veins of leaves and stems of plants. The adults do not move and have a type of scale shell under which they lay eggs. The scales can look like part of the leaf. When the babies crawl out from under the shell, they are transported around by wind, ants or birds. There are various types such as red scale, white louse scale, white wax scale or black scale, some of which secrete honeydew. Scale insects suck the sap from plants and when they are present in large numbers will cause the leaves to yellow and the eventual death of the tree limbs. Treatment: remove any affected leaves and treat the tree with neem oil.

Sooty mould: *fumagina*

Sooty mould is a fungus easily identifiable because of its aptly descriptive name. It feeds on honeydew secreted by insects such as aphids and scale insects and besides looking unsightly it reduces the leaves' ability to photosynthesise. Treatment: sooty mould is a result of other problems so you need to eliminate the underlying cause of the honeydew and the mould will disappear.

Vine weevil: *gorgojo de la vid*

A beetle more likely to attack plants growing in pots than those planted in the ground. It is grey-black, about 10mm long and feeds at night on the leaves of plants. It can be identified by bites around the margins of leaves. Although the damage done does not look particularly attractive, it does not significantly affect the health of the plant. The larvae are the problem: plump white grubs with pale brown heads which feed off the roots and stems of the plants. Once the plant has been badly affected, it will simply fall over and die. Treatment: adults can be picked off plants at night (take a good torch) or trapped with insect barrier glue *(pegamento del insecto)*.

Pesticides and fungicides

No matter how diligent you are, it is not always possible to control pests and diseases. You can keep the trees and plants as healthy and well tended as possible, but sometimes nature works against you. The year 2004 was a prime example with an enormous amount of rain falling very late in spring and creating serious problems in vineyards. The chances are that, at some point, you are going to have to resort to some pesticides and fungicides. Many treatments (such as garlic) may be readily available and easy to prepare, but some are more difficult to obtain. Within the accepted principles of organic farming, some chemicals are permitted. Such chemicals tend to be non-persistent, i.e. active only for a short time, and are reasonably friendly to predators and the environment. The following list contains biological solutions as well as accepted chemicals.

Copper fungicides (Bordeaux mixture and Burgundy mixture)

Bordeaux mixture *(mezcla de burdeos* or *caldo de burdeos)* combining copper sulphate and fresh lime, is used to control diseases of tree-fruits, nuts and vines. A good winter fungicide because it persists through rain. Avoid damaging new plant growth by using a weaker solution in spring, when the tree is budding. Burgundy mixture *(mezcla de borgoña)* is a mixture of copper sulphate and washing soda. Recipes for both these mixtures are available in many organic gardening books and some books on self-sufficiency. I understand the European Union recently passed laws making it illegal for people to use home-produced fungicides and pesticides compounded from copper sulphate. Therefore, I have not included instructions for making these mixes here. However, the use of registered proprietary mixes is allowed.

Derris: *derris*

Derris contains the chemical compound rotenone, a poison that kills a wide range of creatures but is particularly effective in the treatment of fruit flies and aphids. Derris is not a selective pesticide and is only recommended as a last resort.

Garlic: *ajo*

A definite first step in treating aphids and beetles because the ingredients are likely to be close to hand, although the preparation may make the kitchen a little smelly. Crush two bulbs of garlic and add them to one litre of water. Bring to the boil and simmer for 15 minutes. Leave to cool and spray on plants.

Insecticidal soap spray: *jabón insecticidal* or *jabón potásico*

Can be made with biodegradable soap or potassium soap. Pour one litre of boiling water over 50g of potassium soap. Stand for 10 minutes then strain it. Only effective when it comes into direct contact with the insect and only lasts for one day. Slightly more effective than soft soap.

Neem: *árbol de nim*

The neem tree *(Azadirachta indica)* has been used in India since ancient times. In traditional Indian Ayurvedic medicine, the roots, leaves and bark are credited with healing properties and dried neem leaves are mixed with rice and other grains to repel insects during storage. The 20th century saw a rapid growth of awareness outside India of neem's magical properties, an awareness stimulated by Mahatma Gandhi. Neem is believed to fulfil all the priorities within the framework of environmental objectives. It is non-toxic, biodegradable and extremely effective. It is a medium-to-broad-range insecticide effective against almost 400 species of pests and is particularly effective against leaf miners, fruit flies and aphids. Research over the past 50 years has shown that neem does not kill pests but affects their physiology and behaviour, e.g. it can inhibit growth and disrupt mating patterns, although there are some pests out there which may prefer to be a dead pest rather than a stunted, sexless one. In the true spirit of ecology, neem is multi- purpose and manages to be an effective fertiliser.

Pheromone traps: *trampas de feromonas*

Pheromones are natural compounds created in the body and used to communicate with other members of the same species. Traps work by attracting and then trapping pests. Pheromone traps are being used extensively to attract olive fly. They can be either in the form of a sticky pad or a plastic bottle trap. These can be bought but are easily made by putting a liquid containing pheromones into clean plastic bottles, such as empty water bottles, in which two small holes about 1cm wide have been punched on each side of the bottle top. Hung in olive trees, the bottles attract the flies.

Soft soap: *jabón suave*

Only works in direct contact with the insect and only lasts one day. Can be used in conjunction with other sprays.

Sulphur (dispersible)

Organic bodies are still disputing whether this can be classified as organic. It is used to treat mould and rust.

Precautions to take when using pesticides

Spray only on windless days, preferably in the evening.

Protect yourself with suitable clothing, goggles and masks.

Do not put chemicals where children and pets can reach them.

Always follow the instructions on the packet.

Do not spray open flowers as this can harm bees and affect pollination.

Try to target the pest and leave beneficial insects unharmed.

Dispose of all left-over solution.

Wash all equipment thoroughly.

CHAPTER 20
HUNTING AND SHOOTING

Hunting is a popular pastime in Spain both for country-dwellers and weekend visitors. Hardly a public holiday goes by without the sound of gunfire accompanying the dawn chorus, although over the past decade there's been a marked reduction in shooting and an increase in the number of small birds winging their way around the province. However, the latest statistics available for Andalusia, for 2002, demonstrate there is still a high level of interest in hunting. In that year alone 206,587 licences for hunting with firearms were granted, mainly to people in the 38 to 49 age group. The minimum age you can apply for a licence is 14 and within the younger age groups there has been a significant decrease in the number of applications, a possible indication that interest in the sport may be declining.

Hunting is controlled by the *Consejería de Medio Ambiente*, a body which has made great progress in terms of educating the hunting fraternity and controlling the sport. In Andalusia 7,091,289 hectares are registered as hunting land, an unbelievable 80 per cent of the surface area. Of this land, 98 per cent is *coto privado*, or private hunting reserves. The 7,709 reserves are mainly in Córdoba, Granada and Sevilla, Málaga province having the smallest number, 451. The remaining 2 per cent of registered land is classed as "national" hunting reserve. Travelling around the Spanish countryside, you see many signs indicating *Coto de caza* or *Reserva de caza*. These are often accompanied by others showing black and white triangles and an identification number. *Reservas* are generally quite large, covering several *fincas* and parcels of land. Recently, the minimum amount of land required in order to register a private hunting reserve in Andalusia was increased from 500 to 2,000 hectares.

If you are not an *aficionado* of hunting, it can come as a nasty shock to discover that your peaceful property lies in the middle of a hunting reserve and that strangers have a legal right to hunt on your land without consulting you. To many *extranjeros*, it seems a rather upside-down system under which others have rights across your land and it is up to you to apply to limit those rights. Whether you agree with hunting or not, the sound of gunfire echoing over the hillsides on an otherwise peaceful Sunday morning can be quite unnerving. You can't do anything about the noise of the hunters, but if you discover that your land is part of a hunting reserve you do have rights and options. If you do not want hunters on your land, you can establish your rights by fencing your boundaries. For those with a lot of land this can be an expensive business and may not be practical. Apart from this, one of the joyful aspects of the countryside is the sight of large areas of unfenced land and it seems a shame to ruin it with ugly fencing. The alternative is to have your land registered as land to which hunters are denied access. To do this, take your *escritura* and *plan catastral* to your local town hall or office of the *Ministerio de Medio Ambiente* (MMA), which will establish if you are definitely in a designated hunting area and, if so, determine which one. To have your land excluded from a hunting reserve, you have to request the MMA to segregate the area and redefine it as *segregación libre de caza*, i.e. free of hunting.

Hunting Licences

If you wish to hunt or fish, a fairly lengthy procedure is involved. Licences are issued by the *Ministerio de Medio Ambiente*. You must provide evidence of experience of hunting and novices have to take a training course and pass an exam. Most towns and villages have a hunting fraternity which is regulated by a local federation e.g. the *Federación Andaluza de Caza*. These federations organise training courses for hunters and police local hunting reserves to ensure there is no infringement of the law. For some categories of licence, e.g.

hunting with firearms, you will be required to have a medical. You register in the *Registro Andaluz de Caza y Pesca Continental* where you will be given a registration number. Once you have your qualification and registration number, you may apply for a licence, the *Tarjeta de Identificación del Cazador*. If applying for a licence to hunt with firearms, you will also need your NIE and an insurance certificate. To pay the required fee, you take all relevant paperwork to one of the collaborating banks identified on the application form. The amount varies depending on the type of licence, and there is no charge for those over 65.

SAFETY NOTES REGARDING ESSENTIAL OILS

If you are surrounded by many herbs and aromatic trees, it is wonderful to use them to enrich your life in areas other than food or income. Some opportunities for doing this are discussed in each chapter and this appendix aims to provide supplementary information regarding essential oils and their uses.

Essential oils are aromatic essences from plant cells contained in various parts of the tree or plant. There are three main methods of extracting them: distillation, expression and enfleurage. Many of the plants in your garden have natural healing properties which you may wish to utilise. Plants such as Aloe vera only have to be picked and squeezed in order to release the thick green gel that is perfect for treating burns, rashes and sunburn (although it smells rather disgusting). The stems and/or flowers of aromatic plants, e.g. jasmine and rose, can be picked and steeped in oils, such as olive or almond, and then used as a fragrant, moisturising or bath oil.

Distilling essential oils is an ancient and easy process which involves passing steam through the plants to release the essential oils, then cooling and collecting them. Because they are concentrated, essential oils are potent and, used incorrectly, can create problems. They are easily available and reasonably priced here, but it is a little worrying that they can be purchased from many outlets, including street markets, without any safety information.

Essential oils must be used with caution. I have referred to them in many chapters of this book and I would like to stress the following precautions:

Essential oils are strong and can cause skin irritation. Do not use them without diluting them unless you have been advised to do so by a qualified aromatherapy practitioner. They should be mixed with a carrier oil. This can be an oil of your choice, such as almond, olive, avocado, sunflower, or a mix of oils.

Essential oils should never be used on babies or young children nor on people with medical conditions or pregnant women without advice from a qualified person.

Some essential oils are photo-toxic which means that they react to sunlight and can cause discoloration of the skin. This can be a particular problem in Spain where the sun is strong, so be careful.

Essential oils should never be taken internally.

VOCABULARY

Spanish/English

abono: fertiliser
aceite: oil
aceituna: olive
agua: water
alcornoque: cork oak
algarrobo: carob
almendra: almond
arar: to plough
árbol: tree
arbusto: shrub
ayuntamiento: town hall
azadón: mattock
azufre: sulphur

bellota: acorn
breva: young fig

caña: cane
campesino: country person
campo: countryside
castaño: chestnut tree
cáustico: caustic
cavar: to dig
cortar: to cut
coto de caza: hunting reserve

desherbar: to weed
droguería: shop selling
cleaning materials
/chemicals

ecológico: ecological
encina: holm oak
espárrago: asparagus
estiércol: manure

extranjero: foreigner
excavar: to dig a hole
fábrica: factory/mill

fertilisante: fertiliser
ferretería: hardware store
finca: smallholding/country
house
flor: flower
fuego: fire
fungicida: fungicide

granada: pomegranate
herbicida: herbicide
higo: fig
higuera: fig tree
hinojo: fennel
hoja: leaf
huerto: kitchen garden

infusión: infusion

limón: lemon
limonar: lemon grove
limonero: lemon tree

malahierba/mata: weed
malla: mesh
mantillo: mulch
medio ambiente: environment
molino: mill

naranja: orange
nogal: walnut

nuez: nut

perforaciones: drilling (wells)
podar: to prune
pozo: well
propagar: to propagate
plan catastral: plan recorded
in property register

ramo: branch

ramita: twig
red: net
regar: to water
roble: oak
rodrigar: stake a tree
romero: rosemary

sembrar/plantar: to plant
semilla: seed

tijeras de podar: secateurs
trasplantar: transplant

uva: grape

vara: pole
verano: summer
viña/viñedo: vineyard
vivero: garden centre

English/*Spanish*

acorn: *bellota*
almond: *almendra*
ant: *hormiga*
asparagus: *espárrago*

branch: *ramo*

carob: *algarrobo*
chestnut: *castaña*

dig: *cavar*
dig (a hole): *excavar*

ecological: *ecológico*
eucalyptus: *eucalipto*
fertiliser: *fertilisante*
fig: *higo*
fig tree: *higuera*
fire: *fuego*
flower: *flor*

fungicide: *fungicida*
garden centre: *vivero*
grape: *uva*
grapevine: *vid/parra*

harvest, to: *recoger*
harvest, the: *cosecha*
herbicide: *herbicida*
hunting: *caza*

irrigation: *riego*

leaf: *hoja*
lemon: *limón*

mattock: *azadón*
mill: *molino, fábrica*
mulch: *mantillo*

nut: *nuez*

olive: *oliva, aceituna*
olive net: *manta*
orange: *naranja*
organic: *orgánico*

pomegranate: *granada*
propagate: *propagar*

rosemary: *romero*

secateurs: *tijeras de podar*
seed: *semilla*
sulphur: *azufre*

twig: *ramita*

walnut: *nogal*
weed: *malahierba/mata*
well: *pozo*
wildlife: *fauna*

INDEX

USEFUL ADDRESSES

Agriculture, fishing, hunting information:
Consejería de Agricultura y Pesca: general information -
www.juntadeandalucia.es/agriculturaypesca
http://www.juntadeandalucia.es/agriculturaypesca

Hunting & fishing licences information:
cazayupesca.cma@juntadeandalucia.es
mail to: cazayupesca.cma@juntadeandalucia.es

Aromatherapy:
International Federation of Aromatherapists,
Room 8, Department of Continuing Education,
The Royal Masonic Hospital, Ravenscourt Park,
London W6 0TN.

Asociación Agraria-Jóvenes Agricultores (ASAJA),
Mauricio Moro Pareto, 4, Edif. Eurocom Centro, 3ª,
29006 Málaga. Tel: (34) 952 311 111.

Cooperatives:
Confederación de Cooperativas Agrarias de España,
Tortosa, 2, Edif. Mecolleida, 25005 Lleida.

Ecological associations:
Comité Andaluz de Agricultura Ecológica (CAAE),
Cortijo de Cuarto, s/n, 41014 Sevilla. Email: cenfor@caae.es
mail to: cenfor@caae.es
Sociedad Española de Agricultura Ecológica (SEAE),
Partida la Peira, s/n, Apdo.107, E-46450 Benifaio, Valencia.
Tel. (34) 961 788 060. Website: www.agroecologia.net
http://www.agroccologia.net

Environmental Department of Andalusian Government:
Consejería de Medio Ambiente, Delegación Provincial de
Málaga, Mauricio Moro Pareto, 2, Edif. Eurocom, Bloque Sur,
29006 Málaga. Tel. (34) 951 040 058.

Environment and agriculture, provincial delegations of national ministries:
Ministerio de Medio Ambiente and Ministerio de Agricultura, Pesca y Alimentación: Delegación Provincial de Almería, Centro Residencial Oliveros, Bloque Singular, 2ª, 04071 Almería. Tel. (34) 950 012 800
Delegación Provincial de Málaga, Mauricio Moro Pareto, 2, Edif.
Eurocom, 29006 Málaga Tel. (34) 951 040 058.

International Olive Oil Council,
Príncipe de Vergara, 154, 28002 Madrid.
Tel. (34) 91 563 0071. Email: iooc@internationaloliveoil.org
mailto: iooc@internationaloliveoil.org

Organic Gardening:
Sociedad Española de Agricultura Ecologista, Partida La Peira s/n, Apdo 107, E-46450 Benifaio, Valencia.
Tel. (34) 961 788 060
Henry Doubleday Research Association (HDRA), Ryton-on-Dunsmore, Coventry CV8 3LG.
Tel. (00-44) 0247 630 3517.

Permacultura International. Ideas on labour-efficient, small-scale systems of food production and animal husbandry.
Email: admin@permaculturainternational.org
mailto:admin@permaculturainternational.org

BIBLIOGRAPHY

Andalusian Flowers and Countryside, Stocken 1969.
Aromatherapy and the Mind, Julia Lawless, Thorsons 1994.
Aromatherapy A-Z, Patricia Davis, The C.W. Daniel Co. 1988.
Aromatherapy Workbook, Shirley Price, Thorsons 1993.
Complete Book of Fruit, Leslie Johns and Violet Stevenson,
Angus and Robertson 1979.
Culpepper, Nicholas Culpepper, Foulsham.
Discovering the Folklore of Plants, Baker, Shire Publications.
Garden Plants for Mediterranean Climates, Grahame Payne,
The Crowood Press 2002.
Gardening in Spain, Marcelle Pitt, Lookout Publications 1988.
Guía de Campo de Las Flores de Europa, Oleg Polunin,
Ediciones Omega, Barcelona 1982.
Guía de los Plantas Tropicales Silvestres, Enrico Banfi,
Arnoldo Mondadori, Milan 1996.
Holistic Aromatherapy, Christine Wildwood, Thorsons.
Introduction to Permaculture, Bill Mollison,
Tagari Publications 1991.
Mediterranean Gardener, Hugo Latymer,
Royal Botanical Gardens Kew 1990.
Olives - The Life and Lore of a Noble Fruit,
Mort Rosenblum, North Point Press 1996.
Organic Gardening, Ed. Geoff Hamilton,
Dorling Kindersley 1991.
Plants for People, Anna Lewington,
Transworld Publishers 2003.
Plant Propagation, Philip McMillan Browse, R.H.S. 1996.
Practical Gardening On The Costa, Greenfingers,
CB News Publication 2002.
Practise of Aromatherapy, Dr. Jean Valnet,
The C.W. Daniel Co. 1980.
Pruning, Christopher Brickell, R.H.S. Reed International 1992.
Sturtevants Edible Plants of the World,
Dr. E. Lewis Sturtevant, Constable, London 1972.